PRO MOTION

HOW TODAY'S CREATORS BROKE INTO COMICS... AND THEIR ADVICE TO YOU!

PRO
MOTION

HOW TODAY'S CREATORS BROKE INTO COMICS.... AND THEIR ADVICE TO YOU!

BRIAN SANER-LAMKEN
FOREWORD BY MARK WAID

BOARDWALK PRESS
A DIVISON OF SWEET POTATO STUDIOS
WYNNEWOOD, PENNSYLVANIA

ProMotion: How Today's Creators Broke into Comics - And Their Advice to You!
is published by Boardwalk Press, a division of Sweet Potato Studios;
Brian Saner-Lamken, executive editor, art director, publisher, and copy boy.

ISBN 0-9649237-0-X
Library of Congress Catalog Card Number 95-96030
First printing, November 1995
Copyright [©] 1995 Brian Saner-Lamken

Boardwalk Press urges you to support your local comics shop! If, however,
ProMotion is otherwise unavailable to you, copies may be purchased through the
publisher by sending a check or money order in US funds for $17.95 postpaid to
Boardwalk Press, PO Box 362, Wynnewood, Penna. 19096-0362 [Pennsylvania
residents please add $1.05 for sales tax]. Quantity discounts are available for bulk
purchases by qualified retailers, libraries, and educational institutions. Direct all
inquiries to the address above.

*This book is dedicated with love
to Leon and Stella Saner
and to the memory
of Jerome and Mildred Lamken*

Acknowledgments

This book would be much the poorer without the contributions of a great number of people, not least among them the artists, writers, letterers, colorists, editors, and publishers who provided the interviews and essays contained herein. To each and every one, I give my heartfelt thanks, with special recognition due Scott McCloud, for setting such a fine example; Mark Waid, for indulging me in lunch after lunch; and Jerry Ordway and Matt Feazell, for being uncommonly giving of their time and talents.

In addition, acknowledgment is due Nick Bertozzi, Melissa Billings, Stefan Blitz, Adam Cole, Jan Cooper, Rusty Crump, Johanna Draper, Ellen Hurwitz, Tony Isabella, Peter Joe, Robert Longsworth, Russell McDaniel, Keith McKeachie, Kevin Postlewaite, Steven Rappaport, William Schelly, David Schrempf, Tom and Heather Schrempf-White, the membership of CAPA-Alpha, the staff or Fat Jack's Comicrypt, Paul Orkline at Donaldson Printing, Mike Rodor at Professional Duplicating, and most especially Laura Pettit, an editor's editor, for providing friendshi, and support, both material and ethereal.

Last and most, I give thanks to the loving and beloved members of my family. I owe a profound debt to my sister, Jenifer Lamken, for sharing in sidewalk sales and late-night chats; to Herb Cohlberg and Nancy Lamken, for proving that four parents are better than two; to my father, David Lamken, for making sure that I had all the answers; and above all to my mother, Sherie Saner, for teaching me to make my dreams come true, and for leading by example.

It ain't over yet, guys.

Brian Saner-Lamken
October 30th, 1995

Contents

Foreword: "The Icebox Cometh" *by Mark Waid* 1
Preface: "Secret Origins" *by the Editor* 3
Introduction: "Tricks of the Trade" *by the Editor* 7

How Today's Creators Broke
into Comics... And Their Advice to You!

Scott McCloud 13
Dick Ayers 16
Mike Bannon...18
Donna Barr 19
Barry Blair 22
Stefan Blitz 23
Bruce Bollinger 24
Chuck Bordell 27
Mark Braun 28
Roger Brown 30
Kurt Busiek 31
Reggie Byers 34
John Byrne 36
Bruce Chrislip 37
Brian Clopper 38
John Cochran 41
Scott Cohn 42
Terry Collins 44
Randy H. Crawford 47
Howard Cruse 49
Peter David 53
Dan Davis 54
Suzanne Dechnik 55
Sarah Dyer 56
Steve Erwin 58
Michael Eury 61
Matt Feazell 62
Mary Fleener 65
Carl Gafford 66
Rick Geary 68
Nat Gertler 69
Tom Gill 71
Stan Goldberg 73
Steve Hauk 76
Phillip Hester 78

Bob Ingersoll 79
Tony Isabella 81
Gary Kato 86
Barbara Randall Kesel 88
Jeffrey Lang 91
Batton Lash 93
Stan Lee 95
Tom Lyle 96
Stan Lynde 98
John MacLeod 99
David Mazzucchelli 101
Terry Moore..102
Doug Murray 104
Jeff Nicholson 105
Turtel Onli 107
Jerry Ordway 108
Shea Anton Pensa 111
Faye Perozich 114
Gordon Purcell 115
Daniel Reed 117
Scott Saavedra 118
David L. Seidman 119
Don Simpson 122
Evan Skolnick 124
Tom Sniegoski 127
Frank Thorne 129
Jim Valentino 130
Kate Van Zyl/Joyce Slaton 132
Wayne Vansant..134
Neil Vokes...135
Mark Waid 137
Shannon Wheeler 139
Jim Woodring 140
Phil Yeh 141
Ray Zone 145
Brian Saner-Lamken 146

Appendix A: "Making Minicomics" *by Matt Feazell* 150
Appendix B: "What's an Apa, Doc?" *by Rusty Crump*...........................153
Appendix C: "Playing in the Majors" *by Jerry Ordway (with the Editor)*......156

Resources 165
Index 179

PRO MOTION

HOW TODAY'S CREATORS BROKE INTO COMICS... AND THEIR ADVICE TO YOU!

Foreword
The Icebox Cometh
by Mark Waid

The cocktail-party question that I hate most is, without a doubt, "What do you do for a living?"

I don't hate it because I'm embarrassed. Hell, I used to tell *toll attendants* before my girlfriend made me stop snarling traffic. "I write comic books," I tell people with pride, quickly tacking on a list of everybody-knows-*these*-guys credits. "Batman, Superman, the X-Men, Archie…" I tell them that I've been reading 'em all my life. I tell them that I have the best job in the *world*. I tell them that there is nothing else in this world that I ever wanted to *do*. I tell them how lucky I feel every day to do exactly what I *want* to do with my life, nothing more or less.

That's not the part that I hate. The part that I hate is finally having to return with "And what do *you* do?" Because ninety-eight times out of a hundred, I have to pretend that their refrigerator-repairman job is every bit as fascinating as mine.

If you're looking for break-in tips because you think that there's a fortune to be made in comics or because you want to be admired by your peers, buzz off. Go repair a refrigerator. But if you want to tell stories that touch and change the lives of everyday people, young and old, make them laugh and cry and think and know themselves, then push ahead. Push hard and don't let anyone stand in your way, because in this world there's not a more noble profession.

Even for the talented, the comics field is a bear to break into. (Don't go by me, of course; I paid about a dollar in dues and got change back.) But the advice in the pages which follow will absolutely give you a leg up on the teeming competition. No matter *where* your talents may lie - in writing, penciling, inking, lettering, coloring, or some combination thereof - you'll come away from this book knowing more about how to apply them than you do right now.

So go learn. I wish you good luck. All of you except those who will someday come along and put me out of a job…

Preface
Secret Origins
by the Editor

I wrote this book for *you.*

Look, you're reading it, aren't you? You've picked it up, you're browsing through it - maybe you've even bought it, for which I thank you and hope it brings you much insight and pleasure.

It's possible that you're a fan of the creators who have contributed to the book, or that you simply enjoy a good interview, but it's most likely that you have at least a passing interest in - as it says on the cover - how these creators broke into comics, and their advice to you. If you are, indeed, someone who harbors hopes of producing comics professionally, then welcome to the club.

Because I wrote this book for *me,* too.

I've written and drawn my own comics since... well, as far back as I can remember. Other careers were considered along the way, but, looking back, it was pretty much set in the stars that I wouldn't be happy devoting my life's energies to anything else if I hadn't first taken a good, serious walk down this road. I've tried to follow those stars, trusting them to lead me not back to where I began but to someplace new. And they have: I've seen many interesting sights by the roadside, some foreign and some strangely familiar, but I've finally come to a decisive stop on my journey. You're holding it.

Now let me wriggle out of that extended metaphor and tell you how this all started...

I began interviewing professionals in the comics industry back in college, first for academic projects and later for such industry publications as *Comics Buyer's Guide.* Many of the people with whom I spoke were Big-Name Pros, but on occasion I'd meet someone at a convention who, for whatever reason, was utterly unfamiliar to me - and I quickly learned that there are at least three questions that can *always* be asked in such a circumstance: (1) How did you get started in the business? (2) What can you tell [name of publication here] about your current project? (3) Do you have a dream project that you'd like to realize down the line?

The second question is good for the purposes of a timely news or "preview" article, and the third is often an interesting way for the reader to gain some insight into the interviewee. But darn near ten times out of ten, the answer to the first question is what grabs *me*. After all, you'd be hard-pressed to find somebody who's in this business for any other reason than an absolute love for either the medium itself or the way in which it shaped his or her childhood. Creators will speak at length about when, where, and how they first experienced the wonders of the comics page - whether in books or strips - and about just what character, creator, or story moved them to proclaim, "This is what *I'm* going to do."

I'm no different; as I said above, comics have been a lifelong passion of mine, and I can think of nothing, well, *cooler* than getting paid to make them. So I soon began probing that period between a creator's determina-tion to shape the history of his - yes, it's still overwhelmingly "his" these days - favorite hero and his plans for that hero's next big storyline: How did Mr. Pro get his first assignment? What did he do right, what would he do differently, and how can I apply this information towards my own aspirations to *get a job like his*?

Two Octobers past, staring out an airplane window, the title, concept, and format of this book seized my conscious mind. Interviewing profes-sionals from all walks of the comics world had already made me many friends in the industry, and hearing their stories further fueled my own determination to *make it* in this crazy biz. Assembling a book's worth of such stories would not only be a valuable resource to the kids of all ages out there who harbored hopes like mine, but a good way to continue to push *myself* - to keep focused and forward-minded, and to engage in some self-promotion at the same time. And *ProMotion* is just what happened, capital *P*, capital *M* to emphasize the double-meaning of the word.

It soon became obvious that I wouldn't be able to interview enough creators in person, so a few rounds of mass mailings went out. The pages that follow, therefore, are culled both from interviews conducted at conven-tions and via telephone and from forms completed and returned to me via mail; the former necessarily required more editing than the latter, but in every case my goal has been to keep the dialogue as direct as possible from the creator to you, the reader. All conventions of typography are my own, for uniformity's sake, but I believe that in style of writing and speech, each creator's individual voice shines through.

A great many creators were concerned that there wouldn't *be* enough of an individual voice - that their entries wouldn't matter, because everyone would end up saying essentially the same thing. I knew from experience that that wouldn't be the case. But even if it *were*, everyone has a different way of saying that same thing. Many of my contributors do in fact echo one another's advice, and others disagree completely, thanks to the wide *variety* of contributors: The interviews and essays in this book come from all corners of the industry. Some are well-established, having worked steadily in comics for years; others are just beginning. Some "only" draw, or write, or letter, or color, while others create the whole package. The men outnumber the women, just as in the industry itself, but the women are definitely here. The combined body of work of these people runs the gamut of size and shape and fashion, from comic strips to gag cartoons to graphic novels, from slice-of-life to science fiction to frontier drama. Some creators have worked only for the larger, mainstream companies, and others exclusively in the small press; some, in fact, can't even be found in most comic-book stores, preferring to distribute their minicomics and 'zines through a separate network entirely consisting of like-minded creators and fans. *But they're all in comics.*

The world of comics is *not* just about colorful adventures of costumed crimefighters, as prevalent - and as enjoyable - as such stories might be. You don't need crimefighting, you don't need costumes, you don't need adventure, and you don't even need color. You need imagination, and a story, and paper - all of which *you* likely have already; all that's missing is an audience large enough to support your production. That's what "breaking in", a phrase questioned by some of the more independent creators profiled in this book, really means. Admittedly, "breaking in" may imply a club, a room, one specific area of the industry, affiliation with which will legitimize you. And that's not what it's about. "The moment you finish your work and print it up at the local copy shop, you *are* in comics," Scott McCloud told me. Listen to him.

I asked the dean of the minicomics scene, Matt Feazell, to say a few words about self-publishing on a small scale, and he responded by providing the appendix on minis found at the end of this book. That appendix is flanked by two others - one on the benefits to the fan and aspiring pro found in membership to an amateur press association, written by my good friend Rusty Crump, and one taking a very detailed look on how to submit art pages and story proposals to a larger publisher, as revealed in a candid interview with writer/artist Jerry Ordway.

There are many facets to the world of comics, and it's well worth exploring them all. Many creators come down firmly on one side of the fence, preferring mainstream comics to the independent or "alternative" press, and vice-versa. *I* believe that there's room for *both* sides in this industry. Playing in the sandboxes of the larger companies' established superhero universes need not mean selling your soul - but it likely *will* mean that someone else is, ultimately, your boss and the owner of the characters you've borrowed. Creating stories that you own completely, and whose publication and presentation you control, is increasingly easy to do thanks to modern publishing aids - but new, unproven concepts and creators are still met with resistance by all too many factions in the comics marketplace. Both avenues have their hardships, and both have their rewards. And nothing that comes from either side is inherently good or bad simply by virtue of who sent it to the printer. It's all in what's on the page.

I'm well aware that, in the nearly two years between *ProMotion*'s conception and its completion, other books on breaking into comics have appeared on the market. Some deal with matters of style, instructing readers on how to write or draw by certain methods, while others deal very specifically with the professional presentation of stories, scripts, and artwork to publishing houses. In the latter category, Lurene Haines' *Getting into the Business of Comics* is particularly comprehensive and insightful; I highly recommend it to readers looking for a job in mainstream comics.

Why am I plugging the competition? First, because I want you, in your efforts, to explore every possible avenue. Recommendations for further reading are found towards the back of this book. And second, because it isn't really competition: *ProMotion* is unique. Helpful, specific, practical advice is essential and all too rare in this industry, and many of the contributors herein offer such advice - but the *real* focus of this book is on *inspiration*. These creators have pursued their dream and are now fulfilling it. You can, too.

If you were to approach the "me" of three years ago and tell him that he'd have written a book by his twenty-fifth birthday, he'd smile, buy you a Dr. Pepper, and ask you to tell him more. When you got to the part about having published it himself, though, he'd throw you out of the building. But he - that is, I - did it, thanks in large part to the examples set by the creators profiled in *ProMotion*. Much can be accomplished through hard work, perseverance, and sheer force of will.

Now get out there and do it yourself.

Remember, I wrote this book for *you*. The *least* you can do is return the favor...

Introduction
Tricks of the Trade
by the Editor

What gives? A foreword, a preface, *and* an introduction? It is, I admit, almost an embarrassment of riches - but each serves its own purpose: The foreword belongs to Mark Waid; he's there to warm up the crowd before the host comes out, and, despite the refrigerator-repair motif, I think that he's done a fine job. In the preface, you meet the host for the first time. That's *me*. I'll be with you for the rest of the book, so it only seemed right that I give you some insight into what I'm doing here. And now we're ready for the *introduction* - not to me or to the book; we've taken care of that - but to comics.

It's a pretty safe bet that the vast majority of you reading this have at least a passing familiarity with comics. The people whom you'll meet in the pages to come, however, are *intimately* involved with comics. And, on occasion, they might be caught using words and phrases peculiar to the industry that bear explanation. So consider this introduction a primer, an elaborate glossary, if you will. (I never *did* understand why, if glossaries explained so much, they were shoved in the back of the book instead of telling you everything that you needed to know up front.)

First, we need to define **comics**. Those of you who have read Scott McCloud's *Understanding Comics* - and, by the end of this book, you'll realize that that *should* be *all* of you - know that defining comics is much easier said than done, and Scott has already done it better than I ever could, anyway. Scott calls comics "juxtaposed pictorial and other images in deliberate sequence, intended to convey information and/or to produce an aesthetic response in the viewer", though he admits that "sequential art", an oft-used alternative to the word "comics", does nicely in conversation. It's also only fair to Scott to note that the preceding mouthful is conjured up in the very first chapter of *Understanding Comics* largely so that he can get a technical definition out of the way and concentrate on *showing* us what comics is really all about. Be that as it may, I don't have the luxury of Scott's talent, so I'm going to take a brief stab at a definition by shared experience right now - just in case there are still a few of you who bought a book on "breaking into comics" thinking that it had something do with invasive surgery on Jerry Seinfeld…

Think about film. Film tells stories through a series of images - a series of *static* images, in fact; they're just flying through the projector so fast, one after another, that they look like they're actually *moving*. Those static images are essentially photographs - or, in the case of animated films, drawn or painted pictures - called <u>frames</u>. Now imagine a strip of film with certain frames taken out and isolated, placed side-by-side, instead of fed through a projector. You have a comic strip there. (Actually, many movies are planned out as comic strips before they're filmed - only the film industry calls such a strips <u>storyboards</u>.)

A crucial difference between the media of comics and film, though, is how each is able to use the elements of time and space. A film *happens* to you; a comic story is more - to use one of today's biggest buzzwords - *interactive*. You have it on paper, there, in front of you, or perhaps even on a computer screen. The *pacing* of the story - even its *direction*, should you choose to go back and revisit earlier pages before moving on to later ones - is up to *you*. You can't see all of the frames of a film at once, as you can with a comic story in a book or a strip, which is why Scott's definition begins with the word "juxtaposed". It's a crucial word. And for more on the subject, you really should go out and get *Understanding Comics*.

What *isn't* part of Scott's definition, and what I'd like to address here, is the way in which the word "comics" has become *removed* from the definition of "sequential art", or from the longer definition applied by Scott. And to do that, I have to introduce you to my dual definition of the word "medium": A <u>medium</u>, it's generally accepted, is an artistic channel, a way in which a concept or a story or a mood is expressed - through music, through poetry, through film, through comics, through live theater. But the word actually applies to two *kinds* of media - to what I call conceptual media and physical media. Music is a conceptual medium that can be accessed through a variety of physical media, among them compact discs, audiocassettes, and live performances. Likewise, comics is a conceptual medium that can be accessed through comic books, comic strips, and even itself on compact discs or via electronic means on the Internet. While most people think of music when they enter a store that sells records, tapes, and CDs, those physical media aren't exclusive to music, just as music isn't exclusive to them. A spoken-word album is not unheard of. Likewise, items exist that most people would recognize physically as comic books even though they don't actually contain any comics material; pin-up galleries that simply spotlight various artistic renditions of a certain character have recently proven popular, for instance.

This may seem like a purely academic concern, but it isn't. Comics is one of the few media that lends its name to both the conceptual and physical

---

media with which it's associated. And on the pages that follow, the word is used in a variety of different ways. "Comics", when used in the singular, almost invariably refers to either the conceptual medium or the industry that surrounds it - and specifically the comic-*book* industry, as comic books and strips are quite removed from one another in the marketplace. And though it may seem odd to be using a plural as a singular word - which I've been doing throughout this introduction - "comics" is indeed an exception that way. ("Media", coincidentally, is another, as people have become fond of grouping the various facets of the news and entertainment industries into one monolithic entity.)

Despite the name, not everything done in comics has to be humorous, though during the medium's modern birth on the newspaper page, that was the general consensus at the time - hence the naming of the **comic strip**, "comic" simply meaning "funny"; you'll still hear people, on occasion, refer to newspaper strips as "the funnies". But later, as comic strips were collected into book form - sometimes with their panels, the comics equivalent of movie frames, rearranged in the process - the **comic book** was born. Comic strips and comic books diverged a great deal as comic books became increasingly devoted to new material that took full advantage of the larger canvas of the comic-book page, but both are still closely associated in the public consciousness, if not, as noted above, in reality. I use the phrase **comic story** to mean a work of comics as would be found in a comic book. (There also exist upscale-format comic books commonly known as **graphic novels**. To some, the differentiation is one of production values; to others, it's the quality or ambition of work on the pages.)

While some people use the words "strips" or "books" as shorthand to eliminate possible confusion, most people refer to both comic strips and comic books in the plural as, simply, "comics": "Did you read the Sunday comics?" "Our drugstore doesn't sell comics any more." Which physical medium is meant will usually be clear from the context. It will also usually be clear when someone is referring to the conceptual medium, or to the industry, instead: "Comics is a true art form." "I want to break into comics one day." But it still doesn't hurt to know, in advance, that possible confusion lies ahead.

Enough about semantics. What about the nitty-gritty - creativity? Well, you've produced a work of *comics* the moment that you've juxtaposed two pictorial images in deliberate sequence, to return to Scott's definition once again. How are comic strips and comic books made? As you might imagine, that's a tad more complicated to answer, as the procedures vary depending on the preferences, needs, and resources of those involved - but if you'll bear with me, I'll guide you through some common steps.

The true first step in a comic story, as in nearly any creative endeavor, is the **concept** or the <u>idea</u> - which can come from a writer, an artist, a letterer, a colorist, an editor, a publisher, a fan, *anyone*. What happens from there depends on what kind of comic story is being produced, and by how many people. I'll tackle variations on the "usual" course of events as if a different **creator** - broadly defined, someone who lends his or her creative talents to a project - is handling each step.

The initial idea is fleshed out by the **plotter**. Most often, some kind of <u>written plot</u> is established by the plotter; maybe it provides a page-by-page rundown of what will happen in the finished piece, even incorporating bits of dialogue, or maybe it's only a page long altogether, offering just the broadest guidelines to what should happen in the story. To varying degrees, the **breakdown artist** is then left to pace the story, choose "camera angles", and choreograph the action. However, if the plotter is also the **scripter** of the story - which is usually the case - he or she might simply prepare a <u>full script</u> at the outset, instead of a plot - providing for the artist exacting details on how the story is going to progress, page by page and panel by panel, with any necessary <u>dialogue</u> and <u>captions</u> already included.

Conversely, if the plotter of a story will also *draw* that story, a written plot might be foregone completely, with the plotter/artist instead choosing to rough out the plot directly in comics form, going right to the *breakdowns* phase mentioned above - "breaking down" the story into acts and scenes on the page, and placing the characters and scenery, as in a play. An artistically inclined writer might even provide a rough version of break-downs - which are *already* pretty rough - *for* the story's artist, in lieu of a written plot; such breakdowns, rather than being drawn on the heavy art board used for the finished artwork, are commonly drawn up on regular paper, and are often called <u>thumbnails</u>.

Confused? Don't be. The lines between writers and artists in the comics medium blur more than most people realize, since the writing and artwork in comics are so fundamentally interrelated. And many creators work differently from project to project, depending on the preferences of their collaborators and the nature of the project in question.

The first glimpse of the comic story as it will look when printed comes from the **penciler** - who, at least nine times out of ten, was also the break-down artist, in which case the artwork might have gone from breakdowns, or rough pencil art, to <u>finished pencil art</u> without anyone else having seen it in-between. The penciler's job is to define the look of the story, to make the art at once appealing and appropriate for what the story is trying to convey. It's impossible to say whose work on a comic story is most *important*, but the penciler's almost invariably takes the longest to produce.

Once the pencils are complete, copies are made of the penciled pages and given to the scripter. If the plotter and scripter are the same person, and if he or she provided the penciler with a full script, then all that's needed is to make sure that the captions and dialogue from the original script still hold when matched up with the penciler's artwork. On the other hand, if the penciler was provided with a rough plot instead of a full script - or with some hybrid of the two - then the scripter goes back to the computer, typewriter, or legal pad and, based on the art, adds in the words necessary to further convey the story already plotted and drawn. Whichever is the case, the penciler has often built upon *something* in the plot that will suggest new dialogue - or even the excision of dialogue - to the scripter.

(It's important, I think, to remember that comics is a marriage of *writing and artwork*, not of *words and pictures*, as is so commonly misstated; while most comic stories do involve word balloons, captions, thought bubbles, sound effects, and other lyrical additions, they're simply another tool in the toolbox, not a defining element of comics. Here again, comics is like film. Sometimes an actor will keep the audience riveted with brilliant delivery of an impassioned soliloquy; sometimes one choice line is all that's needed to bring down the house; and sometimes a moment of decisive action or quiet calm says more than words ever could.)

With the scripter's job finished, the original pencils and a copy of the script go to the **letterer**, who generally draws the dialogue, narration, and any necessary display lettering - logos, titles, crashes, booms, street signs - right onto the pencilled artwork with black ink; if the pencils are going to be painted rather than inked, however, the lettering is prepared separately and pasted onto a plastic overlay atop the original art. Computer lettering, too, is becoming more common, and applied in nearly as many ways as there are practitioners of the craft.

In general, the closer the story gets to its final, reproducible state, the more sophisticated and specific the artistic tools used. The plotters and scripters can write on whatever makes them most comfortable; the pencilers can use anything from special drawing pencils to a good old yellow number two, as long as it leaves no permanent marks. (Regular, gray graphite pencils have to be erased once the art is inked; blue pencils don't.) **Inkers** and **painters** can likewise use a variety of materials, but they work knowing that their version of the artwork is what will be seen; once the penciled, lettered pages are turned over to them, it's their job to take the infrastructure provided by the penciler and apply the finishing touches. Certain specialized pens and brushes have become standard.

Just as the plotter is often the scripter, the penciler is often the inker - although not nearly *as* often; specialized trades have been a necessity since the earliest days of comics, thanks to publication frequency. If it *is* a case of two-in-one, though, the artist might choose to pencil "loosely" rather than "tightly", knowing what's to come in the inking stage. It's also not unusual for one artist to do breakdowns and another to provide the <u>full finished art</u>, tightening up the pencils and then applying the inks - interpreting the pencils in black, adding texture and depth, enhancing the effects of light and shade - after the lettering has been laid in.

If the comic story in question is to be published in black and white, then inking - including, perhaps, the application of shading using special materials - is the final creative step. Otherwise, that honor falls to <u>coloring</u>, a discipline revolutionized in the past few years by computer technology. In days past, the **colorist** would work on copies of the inked art in markers or watercolor, and then translate his or her work into number/letter codes that called for certain percentages of printers' inks as a guide to the engravers. Now, a colorist often works closely with a **color separator** who can apply more subtle gradations by computer and introduce all manner of visual effects.

At this point in the process, we're far removed from anything that you could approximate at your desk or drawing board at home, and well into an area where you should seek the guidance of a working comics professional; in the meantime, the pages that follow should provide some answers - and further questions - about what your plan of attack should be. The level of <u>production</u> and <u>distribution</u> you seek - what sort of physical form your comics will take when published, and how they'll reach their audience - will depend on your resources and your resolution. As noted in the preface, one of the appendices in this book features a conversation with Jerry Ordway focused on breaking in at the major companies, where the creative process goes something like what I've just outlined, while another features an illustrated guide by Matt Feazell on how to make minicomics - the antithesis of the polished comic books produced by the big guns, and the kind of creativity that might be right up your alley if the above details drove you plumb nutso. It takes all kinds of folks to keep this world hummin' along, and I say, as long as what you're doing feels right to you, *go* for it.

Enough with the prefaces and introductions now. Ladies and gentlemen, without further ado: How today's creators broke into comics... and their advice to *you*.

Scott McCloud

Scott McCloud's award-winning examination of the comics medium, Understanding Comics, *was published in book form by Kitchen Sink, and is currently being reworked as an interactive CD-ROM application. His other work includes the highly acclaimed and thoroughly enjoyable series* Zot! *and the oversized comic book* Destroy!!, *both published by Eclipse, as well as a number of minicomics scheduled for release under the Wow Cool imprint. Currently on Scott's drawing board is a mysterious project titled* The New Adventures of Abraham Lincoln. *Scott was among the very first creators interviewed for this book, and generously allowed his entry to be circulated as an example of what* ProMotion *was all about. As it set the tone in conception, so shall it in publication; everyone else follows in alphabetical order.*

Date and place of birth:
June 10th, 1960; Boston Children's Hospital, Boston, Massachusetts.

First exposure to comics:
Scott was introduced to comics in junior high school by his friend - and future comics writer - Kurt Busiek. "I didn't really have too much interest in them until about the age of fourteen or so," Scott says. "Before that, I really had rather a lot of contempt for comics - I thought that they tended to be poorly done, that they were kid stuff. Kurt began to show me some comics which I thought had a little more potential, and at about fourteen, fifteen years old I actually began to draw some comics of my own. Very quickly, I decided that this was an art form that just fascinated me, that I wanted to experiment with; I determined that I was going to be a comic-book artist, and was very, very single-minded in the pursuit of that goal all through high school and college, until I succeeded."

Breaking in:
"I was trained in illustration at Syracuse University. I had submitted an application to DC Comics' production department, to see if they might need anyone, and they did - Bob Rozakis called me up in my dorm room, woke me up from a sound sleep at nine-thirty in the morning, and asked if I would like to come

to New York for an interview. After some incoherent babbling, I said 'Yes, by all means!' So I went down to New York, I got the job, and three weeks before I left school, I had a job commitment at DC.

"It was really just a day job, there wasn't a lot that was creative about it, but I got to see a lot of the comics world all around me, and the mystique of paper and ink was pretty quickly banished from my consciousness - I no longer saw it as some magical process that only certain select and sacred individuals could do; I realized that it was something that *anyone* could do, including me... not that I didn't already suspect that. And so I began work on a proposal for my own comic series, *Zot!*, which eventually went up to nearly a hundred pages - neatly arranged so that it wouldn't *look* like a hundred pages, thereby not scaring off editors - and I submitted it to several comic-book companies, four of whom expressed an interest, and one of whom, Eclipse, offered what I considered a very good deal."

Advice to aspiring creators:
"It's a difficult time to try to break into comics. There are many more people who *want* to be writing and drawing comics than there are positions open to do so, and the vast majority of opportunities to write and draw comics have been generally very derivative - what I would consider very uninteresting - assignments. It's a very personal decision whether one wants to pursue his or her own style and own idiosyncratic way of making comics, or if one just wants to be a cog in the machine, so to speak. I've been telling people who want to break into comics that just because you've decided to sell out, that doesn't mean that anyone's going to *buy*, and if you're doing something that you're less than enthusiastic about, you'd better be aware of the fact that there are going to be many hundreds of other young artists competing with you who are *not* cynical about what they're doing and who really *do* just want to draw exactly like this year's hot artist for the rest of their lives, and they're going to blow you away.

"You've got to do what you're passionate about, because it's the only way that you can ever compete. Also, if you want to do something which is unique, which is unusual, then you're really only competing with yourself anyway, and the moment that you finish your work and print it up at the local copy shop, you *are* in comics, as far as I'm concerned, and you are very much amongst those of us who care about the medium and are serious about it. You don't really have to wait for someone to give you permission to make comics.

"If you do want to make a career in comics, then certainly one piece of advice is that you'd better be doing *comics*, not pin-ups. Many, many artists come up to me with portfolios full of pin-ups, and while it's very important to learn your anatomy, and to learn the art of making pictures, comics is about much more than that - it's about putting pictures *in sequence*, and that's not a simple art. It requires just as much practice, and just as much discipline, as learning to make the drawings and learning to compose the sentences. That's very important."

Above: A page from Scott McCloud's acclaimed Understanding Comics.
Two pages prior: The title character of Scott's Zot!

Dick Ayers

Dick Ayers' career in comics has spanned dozens of publishers and more than fifty years. He has penciled and/or inked Captain America, The Human Torch, Sgt. Fury, The Fantastic Four, The Incredible Hulk, Giant-Man, *and* The Rawhide Kid *for Marvel Comics;* The Shield *and* The Mighty Crusaders *for Archie; and* Kamandi, The Unknown Soldier, Scalphunter, Jonah Hex, *and* The Freedom Fighters *for DC. Still active at the drawing board, Dick recently illustrated* Chiron, Sorceress of Loutrell *for AnnRuel Studios, and was reunited with a frequent collaborator, the late Jack Kirby, on one of Kirby's last projects, recreating classic early-Marvel covers for auction at Sotheby's.*

Date and place of birth:
April 28th, 1924; Ossining, New York.

First exposure to comics:
Dick was born into the first generation to truly grow up with the comics, and numbers among his early influences Milt Caniff's *Steve Canyon* and *Terry and the Pirates* and Roy Crane's *Wash Tubbs*, two seminal examples of the early days of newspaper adventure serials.

Breaking in:
Dick's first comics job was writing and illustrating the comic strip *Radio Ray* for his Army newspaper in 1942. In 1948, he was assigned his first "civilian" comics job by Magazine Enterprises; fictional, comic-book adventures of Jimmy Durante followed. Early on in his career, he assisted two industry legends - Joe Shuster (the co-creator of Superman) on *Funnyman*, and

Jack Kirby (one of the medium's most prolific and respected artists) on *Sky Masters* and other strips. "I just kept making the rounds, showing samples to editors and publishers," Dick says. "It was Joe Shuster who recommended me to Vin Sullivan and Ray Krank of Magazine Enterprises for the Jimmy Durante book."

Advice to aspiring creators:
   "Concentrate on *storytelling*. It can be *more* important than the illustrating. Comics is a sequential art form. You don't want a page of six panels looking like a poster of collages and montages that the reader needs a road map to follow."

Above: The original Ghost Rider, as rendered by co-creator Dick Ayers. Previous page: Dick's Chiron, Sorceress of Loutrell.

Mike Bannon

Mike Bannon's delightful strip Old Paper *appears irregularly in* Comics Buyer's Guide. *His work has also seen print in* Rip-Off Magazine *from Rip-Off Press and* To Be Announced *and* Jungle Moon Man *from Strawberry Jam Comics.*

Date and place of birth:
June 14th, 1963; somewhere in Dubuque, Iowa.

First exposure to comics:
"When I was a preschooler, my mom bought me a late-'60s *Green Lantern*," Mike recalls. "Shortly thereafter, I started buying comics at the local drugstore. Once I started going to school, I discovered *Peanuts* reprint books in the school library, which really solidified my love of this form."

Breaking in:
"Being an active reader of *Cerebus* led to a lot of cool things happening to me. Around the time that I had a series of oddball letters printed, [*Cerebus* creator/publisher] Dave Sim created space in the back of the book to run 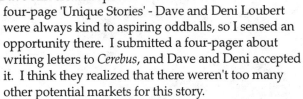 four-page 'Unique Stories' - Dave and Deni Loubert were always kind to aspiring oddballs, so I sensed an opportunity there. I submitted a four-pager about writing letters to *Cerebus*, and Dave and Deni accepted it. I think they realized that there weren't too many other potential markets for this story.

"In turn, through *Cerebus*, I met many friends and had other cartooning opportunities open up to me."

Advice to aspiring creators:
"Well, I think that it's important for a cartoonist to have a life outside of the drawing board. My own goal is to translate my life and twisted outlook into comics - and after years of staying inside and trying to learn how to draw, sort-of, I came to the gradual realization that if I stayed inside all the time, I wouldn't have anything to write and draw about."

Left: Some of Mike Bannon's Old Paper.

Donna Barr

Donna Barr is the creator, writer, and artist of The Desert Peach, *currently published by Aeon Press and available both singly and in collected volumes. Her past work includes several stories for Eclipse Comics'* The Dreamery *and the* Stinz *series from Fantagraphics Books, plus contributions to Fantagraphics'* Naughty Bits *and* Real Stuff, *Caliber's* Negative Burn, *and Palliard's* Xxxenophile. *Donna has also written a* Desert Peach *stage musical, which despite her best efforts might one day end up at a theatre near you.*

Date and place of birth:
August 13th, 1952; Perpetual Health Catholic Hospital, Everett, Washington. "The first thing that I ever did was slug a nun."

First exposure to comics:
"I'm not one of those people who had piles of comics stacked up in my bedroom," Donna says, " although I admit that my brother and I would occasionally sit in *his* room and dramatize his entire three copies of *The Fantastic Four.* The closest that I ever came to collecting comics was the time I clipped out and saved every single strip of Walt Disney's *The Miracle of the White Stallions.* That was because it had horses in it.

"When I was in high school, I picked up two copies of *Enemy Ace,* because it had my *other* mania in it - anything to do with German culture during the twentieth century. The airplanes were beautiful, and the hero, Hans von Hammer, had the most luscious eyelashes on paper, but I kept mumbling to him, 'Geez, Hans, lighten up; do like any *normal* German would do when he's got the blues and go have a *beer.*' I could never find any *other* issues, but as with most comics, if you just read a couple of stories you can extrapolate the rest of the plots, so I wasn't heartbroken.

"I didn't *really* start looking at comics until I began to write and draw them myself, and that's because authors will hand another author free copies."

Breaking in:
"For years I had drawn and written and studied strictly for my own pleasure. My work came to look more like a medieval manuscript, with thousands of words and intricate images crammed onto every one of hundreds of pages. None of it was ever meant to see publication.

"In 1983, I spent some time learning about handmade books, and then minicomics, and changed my style so that it would be more readable. In 1984, I attended a small science-fiction convention, where I offered for sale a homemade minicomic titled *Andri's Christmas Shoes*, with the original *Stinz* story. Steve Gallacci - who had been involved in small press for several years - liked the book, bought a couple of copies, and passed one of them on to Lex Nakashima, a California-based part-time publisher and agent. Lex was my contact with Eclipse Comics, which brought out my first [professional] work in a book called *The Dreamery*.

"*Stinz* was then taken up by Fantagraphics, which published four single issues, and Brave New Worlds, which published two collections. It's been said that I've had more publishers than some publishers have artists. … In 1986, *Stinz* went on the back burner when Steve Gallacci's Thoughts and

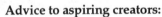

Images brought out *The Desert Peach*, publishing the first three issues. The book was then taken up by Edd Vick's MU Press, later Aeon Press, which continues publishing it today."

Advice to aspiring creators:
"Just keep plugging. Keep drawing, keep writing. Continue to improve your work, and to make contacts.

"Do things a step at a time. If I can get something as unlikely as *The Desert Peach* published, and continue to keep it on the market, and if the audience for such an 'impossible' comic can continue to grow and remain loyal, then there's a chance for *anybody* with talent who backs it with hard work.

"No, I don't think that I'm going to 'hit the big time' for another decade, if then. I don't have any delusions about the accessibility of my work. It takes a long time to build and teach an audience, because there's never been another comic book like mine: It doesn't have a genre, and demands a lot of thinking, on the part of both the writer *and* the reader - but there *are* thinking readers out there, and I'm going to find them. Once they discover my work, they hang on, and I mean to continue producing for them. I haven't been called 'the Gila Monster' for nothing.

"Having the services and support of a publisher as loyal and dependable as Edd Vick doesn't hurt, either."

Above: A panel from Donna Barr's Stinz. *Previous pages: Scenes from Donna's unique series* The Desert Peach.

Barry Blair

Barry Blair is the creator, writer, and artist of Elflord, Samurai, Dragonring, *and other titles formerly published through Blair's own company,* Night Wynd. *He currently writes and illustrates* Elfquest: New Blood *for Warp, and is preparing for* Elflord's *return.*

Date and place of birth:
September 7th, 1958; Ottawa, Ontario.

Breaking in:
Barry began creating his own comic books in 1980, while still working a day job, distributing them to comics shops and bookstores in the Ottawa area as Night Wynd Publishing. Eventually, the books caught the attention of his employer, who, Barry says, "suggested financing a full-scale comic-book series for distribution across North America. We formed Aircel Comics, and in 1985 the first [Aircel] issue of *Samurai* was published and distributed across Canada and the US.

"Being one of the first independent comic-book series of the time, *Samurai* was an overnight success," Barry says. "In subsequent months, I revived other Night Wynd titles, such as *Elflord* and *Dragonring*, which were met with even more favorable response. I have been self-publishing ever since."

Advice to aspiring creators:
"Practice! Practice! Practice! The key to being a good comic-book artist is a combination of drawing well and being able to hit a deadline. Speed and quality come with drawing *constantly*.

"Study the works of non-comic-book artists - Frazetta, Parrish, and Wrightson. Get yourself a good human-anatomy book showing the human body in various stages of running, jumping, etc. Practice sketching the human body in motion. Get some good photo books of different environments - i.e., forests, deserts, city streets, and mountains - and sketch these views to help with your illustration of backgrounds. And finally, don't forget to pay attention to the appropriate shading and textures; this will help give your work depth."

Stefan Blitz

Stefan Blitz's minicomics work includes the irregularly produced Technoboy *series, which Stefan himself adapted for the screen in the short films* Technoboy *and* Technoboy Returns, *and the fumetti book* The Zany Misadventures of Stephen O'Keefe.

Date and place of birth:
April 26th, 1971; Providence, Rhode Island.

First exposure to comics:
Stefan discovered the syndicated *Batman* on TV at an early age, and his first comic book, a DC treasury edition, wasn't far behind. "Growing up in the '70s," he says, " I was exposed to a *huge* amount of reprinted [comics] material, but I had no idea that it wasn't new: In my mind, Spider-Man came alive through Steve Ditko, Batman through Dick Sprang, and mostly everything else through Jack Kirby - until I realized what reprints *were*, and I discovered John Byrne…"

Breaking in:
"As long as I've been able to hold a pencil, I've drawn, and as long as I've drawn, I've wanted to create comics. Along the way, I've been sidetracked by my interests in the film industry, but more and more of the lines between movies and TV and comics are vanishing - and it's all one consuming passion to me."

Advice to aspiring creators:
"Be true to what you feel and what you enjoy. Tell the stories that *you* want to tell."

Right: Stefan Blitz's Technoboy.

Bruce Bollinger

Bruce Bollinger has contributed illustrations to some five-hundred books for most of the major publishing houses. He created a three-issue series, Stranger in a Strange Land, *for Rip-Off Press, and has worked with Doug Wheeler on the* Classics Desecrated *series for Caliber's* Negative Burn. *Bruce cartoons regularly for* Cracked *and its quarterly spinoffs,* Cracked Spaced Out *and* Cracked Monster Party, *and has designed a series of greeting cards for West Graphics.*

Date and place of birth:
April 12th, 1943; Johnstown, Pennsylvania.

First exposure to comics:
"The first I can remember being really turned on to comics is way back in eighth grade, while my parents were stationed in Germany in 1958. I remember spending my entire allowance on those volumes of fascinating stories and pictures, and trading, collecting, and re-trading those comics until I had most of them memorized. The stories fired my imagination and would carry me to places and experiences that I still can sense.

"My allowance went pretty far at the army PX, and by the time we rotated out of the country I had a pile of comics that, when stacked vertically, was taller than *I* was. And, yes, like so many of the sob stories that you've heard before, when we left Germany the weight allowance forced my mother to throw all of my comics away."

Breaking in:
"After I completed the four-year BA program at the Art Center College of Design in Pasadena, California, my wife and I moved back to the Washington, DC, area and I found my first job with a small publishing company doing medical and paramedical books. I made enough contacts during my eight years there to take the chance at freelancing, so in 1976 we moved to the country, lived like hippies, raised our own food, and kept the VW bus running while I did whatever artwork I could find. The work slowly built until I could actually make a living at it. In 1987, I decided to concentrate fully on cartooning and to leave the world of illustration to others. I'd always been told that my illustrations looked funny anyhow, so...

"I presented my concept for a comic book to Kathe Todd of Rip-Off Press and she gave it a shot. During the same time, I tried submitting material to various greeting-card companies, and with moderate success got some of my cartoons on the market. It was at about the same time that Don Martin [one of the cornerstones of *Mad* and later its competitor, *Cracked*] made it known through *Comics Buyer's Guide* that he was needing help; I applied and sent samples - as did a couple-hundred *other* artists - and Don and Norma Martin chose my work.

"I worked on Don's final *Cracked* art for three years, and through the Martins I made contacts at the magazine. When I formally submitted material to the staff, they liked it, and I've been a contributor ever since. I still freelance cartoon art wherever the opportunity presents itself, and it still takes an eight-hour day to make the payments."

Advice to aspiring creators:

"My advice is usually practical, having experienced twenty-five years' worth of art directors and deadlines and decisions. The competition has always been fierce, so you have to be committed to what you're doing *totally*. Don't make your art a hobby, make it a lifestyle. And do it every day. You won't be able to build up the brush mileage, the polish that you will need, by only doing it on the weekends. I still find that if I miss one day at the drawing board, the edge starts to disappear."

Bruce's words of wisdom:

- "Carry a sketchbook, fill it, and get another. Work in black and white at first; leave color until your compositions are strong enough to *use* color. Your work will never look good in color until it is a strong and solid composition in black and white.

- "Draw what is around you as well as the basics of the human form. You live in a body, and you own it, but there are few who can draw one. Even if your objective is cartooning, anatomy and solid form are the first step. Cartooning isn't really a two-dimensional art.

- "Call yourself an artist. It's called 'visualization', and it does work. At first you'll have to give your art away; unless you're an extraordinary artist, no-one will want to pay what you think your creations are worth. Look around the neighborhood, pay attention to what artwork is used around you. Contribute your art when you can - it's exposure, and you never know where it will lead. You will usually find that one effort for little financial gain will lead to someone asking you to do artwork for money.

- "Above all, if you agree to work for someone, *do it*. Do it early and do it to the best of your ability. If you do a half-assed job or do it wrong or do it late, you won't be asked to do another job. This art world is a world of deadlines; get used to it and use them to your advantage. My repeat work comes because my work is done on time the *first* time. The people whom you work with will soon realize that you can be relied on."

Such specfic advice comes from Bruce's own experience in the often cutthroat world of commercial art; it isn't meant to be frightening - merely realistic. In Bruce's words, "An art career is exacting, but ultimately rewarding."

Previous page: The cartoon work of Bruce Bollinger.

Chuck Bordell

Chuck Bordell's credits include inks on Totem, Bloodthirst, *and* E-Man *for Alpha Productions;* Sirens *and* The Marauder *for Caliber Press; and* Dinosaurs for Hire *and* The Protectors *for Malibu Comics.*

Date and place of birth:
March 23rd, 1968; Sharon, Pennsylvania.

First exposure to comics:
"The first comic book that I can remember reading was an issue of *The Incredible Hulk* illustrated by Gil Kane, sometime around 1973 or '74. I drew a few of my own during grade school and sold drawings of Iron Man, Captain America, the Hulk, et al., to other students.

"After a while I lost interest in comics until, in the mid '80s, Frank Miller's *Batman: The Dark Knight* hit me like a ton of bricks."

Breaking in:
"In the late '80s, I sent samples to the major companies and received the standard rejection letters. Some of the letters had comments on them, explaining what the editors thought were my strengths and weaknesses. Changing focus, I sent story proposals and art samples to two small companies, Alpha Productions and Figment Press. I received letters from both companies on the same day saying that they liked my work, and I ended up inking for Alpha and selling a story to Figment Press' *Imago Magazine*. From there, it was a matter of making contact with other editors who had seen my work and proving that I could meet a deadline."

Advice to aspiring creators:
"Learn to take criticism and use it to improve your work without compromising your vision. Submit samples to every company that you can think of, not just the Big Two. And don't - *don't* - imitate another creator."

Mark Braun

Mark Braun penciled Married with Children *and* Slimer and the Real Ghostbusters *for Now Comics and inked Malibu's* Read My Lips: The Unofficial Biography of George Bush. *He took his first stab at self-publishing with* Fanboy Magazine, *and has his own comic-book series in the works. His biggest claim to fame, however, is as a comic-book* character - *Mark was artist Alex Ross' model for Phil Sheldon, the point-of view character in Marvel Comics'* Marvels.

Date and place of birth:
August 9th, 1954; Chicago, Illinois.

First exposure to comics:
"I grew up in a very European household, with my parents upstairs and my grandparents downstairs, along with their son, Ed - my uncle. My parents bought a *Tribune* every Sunday, while my grandfather bought the old *Chicago American* and *Daily News*, so Ed and I would have terrific mornings with *Prince Valiant* and *Gasoline Alley* and *Dick Tracy*.

"Ed and I had a comic-book collection gleaned from other homes - most folks tossed them out - as well as our own purchases: Over a thousand books, from *World's Finest* to *Walt Disney's Comics and Stories*."

Breaking in:
Mark honed his skills early on in a venue familiar to many budding artists. "The high-school paper let me run loose for three years," he says with gratitude, "and it helped get me a scholarship to Chicago's School of the Art Institute. I lasted one year. Lack of direction, I guess."

In 1989, Mark met the art director from Chicago-based Now Comics. "I told her that my daughter loved *Slimer* and that I'd like a shot at a story. So I sent samples, and got a year's worth of work before [Now] went bust. I still work full-time in publishing - when you grow up, you have bills and mortgages - but I still freelance, too. I spent a year self-publishing, which I don't recommend if you're banking on it to make money."

Advice to aspiring creators:

• "Conventions are lousy for real help in comics. Try working up samples and taking a more professional approach by mail *after* you've met [editors] at cons.

• "Developing a personal style is a lifelong pursuit; expect to change over and over again, because just as *people* age and change, so will your tastes and technique.

• "Use caution when doing material that you'll be embarrassed by in years to come. Remember that your audience could run from very young children to aging fanboys with big guts and greasy hair. *Which* audience you cater to is your choice.

• "Don't give up hope and practice, practice, practice!"

Above: A panel from Read My Lips, *written by Matt Tolbert, penciled by Neil Grahame, and inked by Mark Braun. Two pages prior: A Mark Braun-penciled Slimer from* Slimer *and the Real Ghostbusters.*

Roger Brown

Roger Brown has contributed gags to such cartoonists as Don Martin, Gary Fields, John Severin, and Bill Hoest. His comic-book work includes humor material for Marvel's What The—?!, DC's Looney Tunes, Parody's Infinity Charade, *and* Spoof's Tootsie the Dinosaur Hunter.

Date and place of birth:
April 5th, 1957; Munchweiler, Germany.

First exposure to comics:
Roger remembers bringing comic books to school so that he and his friends could trade back and forth "to get to read as many as possible." His mother was responsible for the very first he ever read - and issue of *The Fantastic Four*.

Breaking in:
"I started out writing jokes for a local morning radio show. I enjoyed reading the comic strips in the newspaper and decided to see if they ever bought gags for their characters. The first [gag] that I sold was to Orlando Busino, who does cartoons in *Good Housekeeping*.

"I decided to try sending material to *Cracked*. I was lucky that with my first submission, I sold six pages of material. This led to working with artist Rurik Tyler, who told me that Marvel Comics was looking for writers for *What The—?!* I have been working for Marvel ever since."

Advice to aspiring creators:
"The best advice to creators is to be *persistent* and *professional*. There are a lot of talented people out there who just give up with the first rejection letter that they get. I have a drawer full of rejection slips and form letters.

"I have heard some writers get mad and say, 'I'll show them; I won't send them any more of my work!' They're only hurting themselves. I always try to let the rejection slip make me that much more determined to sell something.

"Editors get large amounts of material to wade through. If your proposal is poorly written and will take the editor a lot of time to decipher, he/she won't *take* the time to read it. By distilling your idea into a few paragraphs, you're making the editors' job easier. If they like it, they will ask for a broader breakdown of the story. Don't give up."

Kurt Busiek

Kurt Busiek's resumé includes such diverse projects as Marvel Comics' Night Thrasher *and Disney's* Mickey Mouse. *He has written* The Legend of Wonder Woman *for DC,* Teenagents *and* Silver Star *for Topps,* Jonny Demon *for Dark Horse, and* The Liberty Project *for Eclipse. Following the success of his and Alex Ross'* Marvels, *he scripted the one-shot* Strange Tales *special for Marvel last year. He is currently at work on* Untold Tales of Spider-Man *for that publisher and his own creation, the exceptional* Astro City, *for Image.*

Date and place of birth:
September 16th, 1960; Boston, Massachusetts.

Breaking in:
In high school, Kurt collaborated with friend and classmate Scott McCloud on an epic superhero graphic novel titled *The Battle of Lexington.*

Regardless of the project's quality in retrospect, it was a bold statement about Kurt's determination; few aspiring artists of any kind see such works through to completion. And his determination has dimmed not at all.

"When I was in college, I took all of the courses I could on scriptwriting and short stories and magazine production - anything that bore any tangential relation to the field [of comics]. As part of a magazine-production class," he recalls, "I was supposed to do a term paper on some magazine and how it worked, and I chose as my subject DC

Comics." Kurt figured the publisher as one large magazine for the purposes of the project, since, for example, advertisements were placed in bulk with multiple titles.

"So I went down to New York City and I interviewed [then-executive editor] Dick Giordano, and while I was talking to Dick, I told him that I was an aspiring writer, and asked him how I would go about breaking in. When you ask an editor that, the editor will [usually] tell you to send story premises, no more than a page, double-spaced. Dick must not have been thinking that day, because Dick said, 'Write some sample scripts and send them to me, and I'll read them.' So I went home and shortly before the end of my senior year I wrote four full scripts for DC Comics characters - a Supergirl story, a *Superman: The In-Between Years*, a *Flash*, and a *Brave and the Bold* with Batman and Green Lantern - and I sent them to Dick. Dick didn't have any time to read them - nobody in that kind of position has time to read spec stuff like that - but at the same time he had asked for them, so he couldn't very well say, 'Well, I really don't have time, sorry.' So he gave them to the editors for which books they were written - and instead of *me* sending them to the editors, the editors got them from their *boss*, who said, 'Here, read these.'

"The editor of *The Brave and the Bold* never got around to reading that script, but Julius Schwartz and E. Nelson Bridwell read the Superman and Supergirl scripts, and I did a sample Superboy script [for them] that never got anywhere. Ernie Colón was the editor of *Flash*, and he liked the Flash script enough to have me do a *Green Lantern Corps* story; I did a couple *more* stories for him, and by that time, [Marvel's] *Power Man/Iron Fist* needed a writer, so I sent a sample plot in to Denny O'Neil, with the magic words on it, 'I've already sold scripts to DC.' Denny needed a writer and he liked my stories, so he hired me and I ended up being the regular writer on *Power Man/Iron Fist* for a year.

"That's how I broke in. At each step, I was able to say, 'Look, I did this,' and all because Dick made a mistake."

Advice to aspiring creators:
"Don't give up. If you can work for the smaller companies, and the bigger companies aren't giving you the time of day, then work for the smaller companies. If what you really want to do is work that you own yourself, then aim yourself at the publishers who *do* that kind of work.

"The thing that anyone who's trying to break in out there has to understand is that comic-book editors do not, by and large, have to find new writers, new artists, whatever. What they have to do is fill their books. And unlike the editor of *Playboy*, who has to fill the magazine with articles and interviews and so forth by different people every month, the editor of

Captain America knows that Mark Gruenwald is going to be writing it every month; and if Mark quit, then he's going to look around first at the ranks of established writers [which he did - Mark Waid now writes *Captain America*]. So an editor at a book publisher is *always* looking for new writers, an editor at a magazine is *always* looking for new writers, but an editor at a comic-book company is only *sometimes* looking for new writers. And that is why the job isn't structured around looking for new talent.

"It's enormously hard, but the thing that a 'would-be' needs to do is to understand what it's like to be behind the desk: Nobody wants to hire you because you want a job; they want to hire you because you can give them something that they don't have. So the editor of *What If?* is the editor who needs a different writer every month. The editor of *Showcase* is somebody who is *specifically* looking for new writers. *Marvel Comics Presents* regularly had new people coming in. Whether it's established people or new people, they're people who weren't working on the book last month. So those are the books to target, those are the books to look at."

Above: Brent Anderson art from Kurt Busiek's Astro City. *Two pages prior: Alex Ross' rendition of the Human Torch from the award-winning* Marvels.

Reggie Byers

Reggie Byers currently writes, illustrates, and publishes his creation Kidz of the King, *a religious superhero series that reflects Reggie's own spirituality and Christian beliefs. His past projects include* Robotech: The New Generation, *which he penciled for Comico, and* Shuriken, *another of Reggie's own creations, which he drew first for his own company, Victory, and later for Eternity Comics.*

Date and place of birth:
May 19th, 1963; Charlotte, North Carolina.

First exposure to comics:
An *X-Men* fan for life, Reggie was also captivated in his younger days by a variety of Japanese cartoons, including *Star Blazers*, *The Eighth Man*, and *Kimba the White Lion*.

Breaking in:
"I lived in Norristown, Pennsylvania, where Comico - the original version - was located, and when I first heard of it I approached the people there with my work. They were impressed, but they really didn't have any openings artwise, so I started working in their office, doing whatever. At the same time, I was also going to art school in Philadelphia, taking illustration and commercial-art courses."

Reggie had been working for Comico nearly a year when the publishers got the rights to produce comic books based on the popular Japanese animated TV series *Robotech*. "Since they knew that the majority of the work I enjoyed doing was of the *manga* [Japanese-comics style] variety, they gave me a shot at one of the books. That's how I got my start. It was really a blessing."

In 1987, Reggie entered the world of self-publish-

ing with *Shuriken*. "Rich Rankin, who inked every issue that I did of *Robotech*, left Comico the same time as I did, and we each got into self-publishing; I did *Shuriken* under the Victory logo, and he did *Eagle* - which was like a male version of *Shuriken* - under the Crystal logo.

"Victory went out of business after about two years. I was just not being consistent. At the time, I was young, I took everything for granted, I wasn't a real businessman - not that I'm a real one now, but I have some experience under my belt and I know what to avoid. After Victory, I took *Shuriken* over to Eternity Comics; they took care of the publishing, and I drew it for them. After awhile I just got so disillusioned with the whole scheme of the comics industry that I left it totally and sold *Shuriken* to Eternity. I got married, opened up two airbrush shops, and now I'm ready to get back into comics again."

Advice to aspiring creators:
"If you're interested in getting out there, what you have to do is keep working hard on your art style, figure out your look. Look at different comic books, check out the styles and the techniques. Study the things that some people may not feel are very relevant, like anatomy, perspective, color, and design, because all of these things that are taken up in art school are very important in creating comics. I think that drawing from life helps as well - sitting outside and drawing the trees, or drawing a family member while they're sitting still watching TV. Drawing from life helps a person's work be more limber, more convincing, than drawing from comics, which ends up static.

"When it comes to self-publishing, you need to make sure that you feel there's an audience for what you're doing. If you're self-publishing, it's most likely going to be black and white - and if it's just a superhero in black and white, chances are that it's going to fail unless your artwork is really, *really* out there. Target an audience, *then* concentrate on your work."

Previous page: Zeal, Mercy, Truth, and Faith - Reggie Byers' Kidz of the King.

John Byrne

John Byrne became a fan favorite for his work on Marvel's X-Men *and* The Fantastic Four, *and redefined Superman for DC a decade ago in* The Man of Steel, Superman, *and* Action Comics. *His creations* Danger Unlimited, The Torch of Liberty, Babe, *and* John Byrne's Next Men *have all been published under Dark Horse Comics' Legend imprint. John currently writes, draws, and letters DC's* Wonder Woman.

Date and place of birth:
   July 6th, 1950; Walsall, England.

Breaking in:
   John worked for a number of fanzines, including *Epoch*, *Chronicle*, and *CPL* *(Contemporary Pictorial Literature)* before turning pro. His first published work appeared in *Giant-Size Dracula* at Marvel - a short story written by Tony Isabella - and soon thereafter his and Nick Cuti's *Rog-2000* appeared as a back-up in Charlton's *E-Man*.

Advice to aspiring creators:
   "Learn to draw, then learn to draw comics.
   "Learn to write, then learn to write comics."

Right: John Byrne's version of Wonder Woman.

Bruce Chrislip

Bruce Chrislip is a minicomics veteran whose work has also appeared in Aardvark-Vanaheim's Cerebus Bi-Weekly *and Kitchen Sink's* Images of Omaha. *He self-publishes the oddball anthology* Paper Tales *under the CLG Comics imprint.*

Date and place of birth:
November 10th, 1954; Youngstown, Ohio.

First exposure to comics:
Like so many of us did back before specialty shops came into existence, Bruce discovered comics at the corner drugstore. "It had a wonderful little comics section," he says of his old haunt. "My two older brothers read comic books and I started buying them before I could even read."

Breaking in:
"An associate of mine was the editor of *Giant-Size Mini-Comics* #4 for Eclipse. I contacted him and asked to be in the book, since it was a multi-artist anthology title, and he agreed to put me in - so asking for the job *can* work. Of course, prior to this, the editor had seen my work in numerous minicomics."

Advice to aspiring creators:
"Get your work seen first. Do minicomics. Build up a portfolio of printed work. Approach the bigger companies *only* after you've paid some dues, after you've learned how to do comics by drawing for the small press.
"When you're 'ready for prime time', approach companies at comic-book conventions. Whatever your comic-book interest, try to be original. Your drawing style is your handwriting; copying another's handwriting amounts to forgery.
"Last but most important: Learn to deal with rejection. All cartoonists have to face it, even longtime pros."

Above: A panel from Bruce Chrislip's Paper Tales.

Brian Clopper

Brian Clopper began his comics career with Partners in PanDEMONium, *published by Caliber Press. Since then, he has drawn a* Classics Desecrated *story for Caliber's* Negative Burn *and both written and illustrated a short* Fiend *story for that same series. He is currently at work on a humorous fantasy novel, titled* Know-It-All, *and* Fever Pitch, *a comic-book series that he plans to self-publish.*

Date and place of birth:
September 6th, 1967; Hagerstown, Maryland.

First exposure to comics:
"It was in middle school that I started to pick up comics - I was a huge science-fiction fan and way big on *Star Wars* at the time. A few close friends and I had a spaceship-drawing club. Every morning in homeroom, we would evaluate each others' drawings. One guy was great at ship-wrecks on exotic, alien planets, while the other was good at interstellar battles and explosions. I, however, specialized in spaceships.

"Suitably enough, my first comic book was *Star Wars* #38, featuring the profoundly excellent art of Michael Golden. Ever so slowly, I began to pick up other titles and, pretty soon, I was hooked. Gastrointestinally speaking, collecting comics was rather intrusive: My lunch money was hardly ever used in the dreaded cafeteria. Instead, it became useful capital to be invested at the comics rack."

Breaking in:
"I sent out my first proposal, *Partners in PanDEMONium,* to various publishers shortly after graduating from college, and I received polite rejections from all except Caliber. I was excited and revved up to do the series. I had ideas pumping through my head that would've kept the series going for twenty issues or more. Unfortunately, my book was released around the time when retailers, having been burnt by the black-and-white implosion [a time when the comics market was saturated with indepen-dent, small-press black-and-white books], were reluctant to order an obscure book by an unknown. The orders on *Partners* dropped below the break-even point and the book had to be canceled. This was very frustrat-ing because I had heard fellow professionals responding very positively to the book. Reluctantly, I grinned and bore it.

TRUE, BEING AN ARTIST HASN'T PROVEN TO BE THE MOST LUCRATIVE CAREER PATH—

—BUT IT'S SOMETHING I FEEL I GOTTA DO!

"Shortly after *Partners*, I landed a series, *BratterSkain*, with a new publisher, Comic Zone. Two issues of the book were completed, along with the covers and scripts to all three issues. The book even got a spotlight in [Diamond Comic Distributors' solicitation catalog] *Previews*, but, alas, orders came in too low. This was a telling blow. Riddled with doubts and insecurity, I dropped out of comics as a vital creator. I continued to work for Insight Studios, doing such frustrating odd jobs as paste-up, lettering, and background inking. I eventually worked up several more proposals and sent them off to various publishers, but no-one was looking to do anything beyond the standard superhero fare. My projects tend to delve into the contrast between the mundane issues of life and the ornate tapestry of fantasy and myth.

"[Last year] I completed my certification as an elementary-school teacher and have since begun teaching. I took the jump into full-time employment so that I could approach self-publishing with a degree of financial confidence. I intend to spend the next couple of years refining my storytelling skills, so that when I self-publish *Fever Pitch* it will radiate a deeper personal commitment and confidence."

Advice to aspiring creators:

"The following advice is something that I learned the hard way.

"I thought that doing the work at the drawing table was all there was to the comic process. I have since learned that being shy and gracious gets you a one-way ticket to obscurity. You have to go out and not only *sell* yourself but *share* yourself. Honesty and sincerity about your project works staggering magic. The delicate area lies in not getting overly cocky; no-one likes a crass braggart.

FOLKS AROUND
HERE CALL ME
LIL. YOU MIGHT
KNOW ME
BETTER AS
LACHESIS.

"One of the most significant things that you can do for yourself, especially if you are going to self-publish, is to be involved in your work. Don't just ship the finished art to the printer and go on to the next issue. It's vital that you stand behind your creation. Store appearances are crucial. Develop strong ties to the retailers and public. Get people excited about your book. A loyal following that senses a creator's enthusiasm and commitment will spread word of mouth at a tremendous rate. Look at the wonderful success of *Bone*. Jeff Smith's book proudly beams uncompromising integrity and trust.

"Marrying a profusely supportive woman also helps."

Above and previous page: Scenes from Brian Clopper's series Partners in PanDEMONium.

John Cochran

John Cochran has written for Warren Publishing's Eerie, *and he spent a year as that company's editorial director. His articles on comics have appeared in* The Comics Journal *and numerous other publications.*

Date and place of birth:
   March 15th, 1943; New York, New York.

First exposure to comics:
   "The first comic book that I remember was a Terrytoons comic book - *Heckle and Jeckle, The Talking Magpies.* That was when I was all of four or five, and I've been reading comics ever since."

Breaking in:
   "I besieged Warren Publishing czar Jim Warren; he started me out on a freelance basis, and then hired me full-time. Working for Warren was not all peaches and cream, but I'm glad that he gave me a shot at it."

Advice to aspiring creators:
   "Hang in there. Try like hell to be original. Don't recycle the tried and true. Study the great comics of the past - *Dick Tracy, Plastic Man, Captain Marvel,* the early Marvel comics. Try to remember that you're supposed to be telling a story, not just showing off."

Above: A panel from a classic Eerie *story drawn by the legendary Steve Ditko.*

Scott Cohn

Scott Cohn has contributed pencils to issues of Marvel Comics' Quasar *and* Claypool's Phantom of Fear City, *and illustrated an entry in the anthology* The Big Book of Urban Legends *for DC's Paradox Press imprint.*

Date and place of birth:
   January 11th, 1974; Philadelphia, Pennsylvania.

First exposure to comics:
   "When I was about five years old, my babysitter, Kevin, read comics, so I started reading them too. At age seven, I decided that drawing comics was what I wanted to do when I grew up. I drew for hours every day for years, copying, tracing, and doing my own stuff."

Breaking in:
   Scott's first pro work came during his sophomore year at New York's School of Visual Arts, thanks to SVA instructor and comics veteran Joe Orlando. "I met with him at DC Comics one day and was introduced to Andy Helfer, through whom I got *The Big Book of Urban Legends*," Scott says.
   "For two years before that and up until now, I've been an inking assistant for a few people - but if I told you who they were, I'd have to kill you."

Advice to aspiring creators:
   "Don't bother. The less people who are trying to get work, the easier it is for me.
   "Ahh, come on, I'm not *that* much of a jerk!...
   "I'm gonna say what everyone *else* is gonna say: Draw from real life - anatomy, buildings, cars, apples, bugs, guns, wrinkles in clothing, etc. Comics are about more than just muscles, crosshatching, and speed lines. You have to think of this business as a *craft*, and not something that's done just for fun, whether you can draw or not. I think that that's why the industry's at a low point right now. ... The thing that you have to understand - and this is something that I didn't get until a few years ago - is that there's a *science* to drawing comics. It's not just big fancy drawings on a page. It's very hard when you're starting out, because it feels so overwhelming, to think of everything that you should and shouldn't do. I'm still trying to figure it all out. Storytelling is very hard, and it seems like it's rapidly becoming a lost art.

"If you can hook up with someone in the industry, that's a godsend. In my case, I've made friends with quite a few big names in the industry, and their advice has been invaluable to me.

"Make contacts at comic-book companies. If you can get into the offices and talk to editors and get them to look at your stuff, *do it*. But don't be a [nuisance] about it. If you do a mailingto editors, call in after a few days to see if they got it. Ask what they thought, but, again, don't be a [nuisance]. You're selling *yourself*.

"And lastly, learn how to use a computer. The industry's getting bigger and bigger because of them. You want to ride the train, not watch it leave the station."

Above: Scott Cohn's rendition of the Batman and friends.

Terry Collins

Terry Collins' work has appeared in a electic array of books from a number of publishers - among them Millenium's Doc Savage, *Innovation's* Lost in Space, *Archie's* Jughead, *NEC's* The Tick: Karma Tornado, *Marvel's* The Ren and Stimpy Show, *and DC's* Tiny Toon Adventures. *Terry is currently the monthly writer for Warp Graphics'* Elfquest: Blood of Ten Chiefs *and, with artist and co-creator Bill Neville, is self-publishing* Explorers *through Explorer Press.*

Date and place of birth:
June 11th, 1967; Mount Airy, North Carolina.

First exposure to comics:
"My first exposure to comics came from my grandmother, who bought me an issue of *Dennis the Menace* when I was four years old," Terry remembers. "I was instantly hooked. Since I actively read everything that I could get my hands on, comics were just part of a routine that included science fiction, *Doc Savage, Mad* paperbacks, *Rolling Stone,* and mystery/suspense novels. ...

"I was lucky [that] my parents never had a problem with my collecting comics. My neighborhood was full of comic-book fans; we all actively traded back and forth - and, as a result, I was exposed to a wide variety of titles that I could never have afforded otherwise. I was also enthralled by the *history* of comics and read and re-read any information that I could find on comics creators. I always knew that I wanted to work in the field; it was just a matter of when."

Breaking in:
"During my college days, I had sent original mini-series concepts to various editors in hopes of getting published. I knew enough about professional writing to submit well-written cover letters and concise overviews of what I had

in mind, so I was probably ahead of the game compared to other aspiring comic-book scripters. Some of these pitches were with an artist friend who provided illustrations, and others were solo. This was the mid-to-late '80s, and an unknown writer could still break in at one of the smaller companies with a fresh idea.

"Initially, I received polite rejection letters with invitations to send more samples from such people as Diana Schutz at Comico and Will Shetterly at SteelDragon Press. This was encouraging, and I kept at it, with some minor success placing short stories and one-pagers in various anthology titles.

"In the fall of 1989, Innovation expressed interest in an original three-part mini-series of mine and contracts were signed. The series was never printed due to the company-assigned artist leaving the project - but my name was now known in the offices, and I was invited to submit to Innovation's comic-book revamp of *Lost in Space*.

"At approximately the same time, I had contacted then-Millenium editor Mark Ellis about possibly submitting story ideas in person. I had noticed that Millenium's offices were in Florida, where my wife and I were planning our vacation. Mark was gracious enough to meet with me. He read my samples, and liked them; we hit it off, and soon after I was offered an assignment on Millenium's upcoming horror title *HP Lovecraft's Cthulhu*, which began a four-year stint of working for the company. From then on, it became easier to approach editors since I had credits and could present published work."

Advice to aspiring creators:

"Writers are readers. Read novels, non-fiction, magazines, and, yes, comics. Read lots and often. However, since you *are* writing for a visual medium, watching movies and television with a critical eye to gain a stronger cinematic sense is also useful. You'll be amazed at what you see if you're paying attention.

"Talk to other writers. Drop them a letter, or, better yet, approach them in person at conventions. Most writers aren't exactly deluged by hordes of fans demanding a sketch, so they'll appreciate the attention. Give them a sample of your work to take home and critique. Most writers will be glad to do this - just don't expect a speedy reply.

"And while you have a writer's attention, inquire about purchasing a photocopy of one of his or her scripts. Obtain scripts from lots of different writers to see what techniques working professionals are using. Format, style, layout - all can be seen in an original script. Compare the script to the finished comic book. Very enlightening.

"When submitting an idea for an established character from one of the major publishers, keep it short. If you have a plot for a fill-in issue of

NO, WHAT I NEED IS A DIVERSION.

Spider-Man, take no more than a page to set up your story from beginning to middle to end - double-spaced. As insulting as it may appear, editors at Marvel and DC are buying ideas, not writers.

"Also, be aware that submitting story ideas for *Spider-Man* is a waste of time for a new writer. The same goes for *Batman*, *X-Men*, *Superman*, and any other major title. If you *are* interested in work-for-hire, set your goals lower and go for lesser-known books. Remember what Alan Moore did with *Swamp Thing*.

"Always keep in mind that comic-book scripting is an invisible art form. The public at large never sees your writing - it only sees a final collaborative creation, and most of the time it's going to be drawn to the visuals. This is why a writer's teeth always grind when asked 'What book do you draw?' Joe Public understands writers when it comes to television and plays, but the concept of 'writing for comics' is beyond him.

"To add to the fun is the deluge of pencilers, inkers, letterers, and colorists who all want to write, which increases the competition in an already crowded field. They already have the ear of the editor - who, more often than not, is *also* a writer. The only way to circumvent this caste system is to be a better writer than the competition.

"It *is* possible to break into the business by sending in submissions over the transom. I did it, and so can you. Be prepared for rejections, but don't let a form letter stop you. Successful writers are usually both talented and stubborn. Keep trying and learn from each submission.

"Self-publishing is enjoying a boom right now from creators who are frustrated with the limitations of work-for-hire. If you have an idea for a series and want to keep it pure, find a like-minded artist and publish your own title. The financial end may be smaller, but the creative rewards are much more satisfying."

Above: A Bill Neville-drawn panel from his and Terry Collins' Explorers.
Two pages prior: The Tick, as rendered by creator Ben Edlund.

Randy H. Crawford

Randy H. Crawford is the creator of numerous minicomics, produced alone and in collaboration for various small-press publishers, including his own Nice Day Comix. His work has also appeared in Palliard Press' Xxxenophile and Jabberwocky Graphix' Goodies. Randy currently produces the groovy monthly newsletter for the Wyoming, Michigan, comic-book store Between the Covers.

Date and place of birth:
January 16th, 1953; Butterworth Hospital, Grand Rapids, Michigan.

First exposure to comics:
"Attracted by the similarity to TV animation, I was a pre-literate fan of comic books and newspaper comic strips," Randy says. "I got an early start at learning to read by asking my mother to explain the writing in the bubbles to me."

The rest of Randy's family helped out as well: "I have distinct early memories of trudging anywhere from two-and-a-half to twenty blocks to various area drugstores to buy comics, occasionally in the deep snow. Specific early comics memories include my half-brother buying me the second Silver-Age Flash comic at a corner drugstore and my father buying me *Fantastic Four* #6 and early-'60s *Mad* magazines at the supermarket. I also recall choosing a Batman comic - in preference to a candy bar - bought by my aunt, who later taught me how to draw."

Breaking in:
"Oddly enough, it's been by invitation all the way.

"In 1976, I met Ronnie Lane at a party, and he asked me to illustrate *Man Unleashed upon the Universe*, the first comic that I ever drew, for Free Books. In 1978, I received a phone call from Scott MacEachron; this led to my first self-published book, *Nice Day*. In 1980, Howard Shanken, then of Morgan's Mopeds, asked me to produce *The Adventures of the Moped Cowboy*. In 1985, Rober Koopmans, my fellow employee at the Book Stop of Wyoming, Michigan, asked me to collaborate on my first minicomic, *Bolt, No Further Adventures*. After that, I began publishing *Nice Day Mini-Comix* on a quarterly basis up through #20, and sporadically since.

"Going 'pro' worked the same way: I sent a fan letter in comic-strip form to Brad Foster of Palliard Press; he replied by asking if he could cut it up and publish it. It appeared in *Goodies* #46. When the first issue of

Xxxenophile appeared, several months after my own hardcore short-story anthology *Plain Brown Wrapper Special* #2, I wrote to Phil Foglio expressing my admiration for his work, and he hired me to ink a short piece which appeared in *Xxxenophile* #3. I *still* don't know who got me onto the invitation list for Fantagraphics' *Amazing Heroes Swimsuit Special*, but both times they invited me to submit something I sent in eight cartoons and both times they used four of them."

Advice to aspiring creators:

"If you have the talent and determination to work very hard at improving, if you can bear the rejection, if you really need the money, and if you're willing to learn to hate doing what you once loved and then keep on doing it anyway, thanklessly, with no job security or future, then by all means become a comic-book professional.

"*However*, if you'd rather write and draw whatever you want - as long as it isn't libelous or obscene - in your own distinct style without any editorial or corporate interference or restrictions, and as long as the necessity to make a profit isn't a serious consideration, then the near-limitless freedom of self-expression open to you through small-press self-publishing is worth your *serious* consideration."

Above: Egor and the gang from Randy H. Crawford's Egor's Hobby Hints, *all dressed up with no place to go.*

Howard Cruse

Howard Cruse's work has appeared in such diverse magazines as Playboy, The
Village Voice, Heavy Metal, American Health, *and* Starlog. *He is perhaps best
known for the comic strip* Wendel, *which appeared in* The Advocate *fo six years
and has since been collected in two volumes; his latest book is* Stuck Rubber Baby,
*released this year by Paradox Press. Howard was inducted into Chicago's Under-
ground Comix Hall of Fame in 1993, the same year that he won the Stonewall
Award for activism on behalf of lesbians and gay men.*

Date and place of birth:
May 2nd, 1944; Birmingham, Alabama.

First exposure to comics:
"I discovered *Little Lulu* when I was five, and I was hooked."

Breaking in:
"'Breaking in' has amounted to a seemingly neverending trek through
the wilderness, during which a million 'baby steps' have been punctuated
by very occasional and very limited
'leaps forward'. My first published
comic strip, *Calvin*, began running in
our county newspaper when I was
thirteen, if memory serves. Around
the same time, I sold my first single-
panel gag cartoons to *The Baptist
Student*, a regional publication, and
had my first national exposure in a
truly awful *Mad* imitation called
Fooey. While I was in college, I sold a
piece to *Sick Magazine*, and contributed satirical gag cartoons to my
college newspaper and political
cartoons to the Shades Valley *Sun*, a
suburban weekly. I also spent the
summer of 1967 working as a staff
artist at the Birmingham *News*,
where regular illustration assignments permitted me to hone my

cartooning style. The first appearance of a 'real' Howard Cruse comic strip
- that is, one less derivative than previous efforts, representing the first
glimmers of a mature perspective inspired by my own life experience -
came in 1969, when my strip *Muddlebrow* appeared briefly in a weird quasi-
feminist New York weekly called *Granny*. In 1970, I began drawing *Tops and
Button*, a funny-animal cartoon panel that appeared daily for two years in
the Birmingham *Post-Herald*. In 1971, I launched *Barefootz* as a twice-
weekly strip for the University of Alabama *Crimson-White*. I continued
thereafter to draw *Barefootz* for assorted underground newspapers published in the Birmingham area. Eventually I sent a package of those strips
to Denis Kitchen at Kitchen Sink Press. He liked them, reprinted a few, and
encouraged me to do new episodes expressly for his *Commies from Mars*,
Snarf, and *Bizarre Sex* series.

"Want to copy my system? *Fooey* and the St. Clair County *Reporter* are
long gone, but *The Baptist Student* may still be looking for contributors..."

Advice to aspiring creators:

"While you're waiting for Marvel or Fantagraphics to recognize your
genius and give you a monthly title, get your work into print however you
can, wherever you can, no matter how little you're paid. In other words,
unless you're unusually lucky it's gonna be that day job that keeps your art
[career] afloat for quite a while.

"Don't turn up your nose at that supermarket giveaway or tenants'
newsletter. You must have the experience of reaching an audience and
checking out how your ideas and/or drawings are going over. In time
you'll have samples with which to impress more discerning editors of more
professional publications. But still, be prepared to work cheap in the
beginning. It's worth it to learn how your own evaluation of your work
squares with the opinions of editors and readers who do not know you
personally, have no interest in flattering you, and care only about your
capacity to communicate effectively with them and entertain them.

"Copyright everything that you do in your own name, whenever
possible. These days it's practically as easy as drawing a circle around a 'c'.
Do a little research to nail down an understanding of current copyright law.
You'll be glad that you did.

"As your early stuff begins seeing print, chances are that you'll discover
you're a lot less brilliant and graphically skilled than you think you are.
This is a very important insight; you will never learn to look at your own
work clearly and devise strategies for improving it until you get past
lingering childhood illusions that you're already as good as you need to be.

"Getting repeatedly dashed in the face with cold water will never be fun,
but it's necessary for artistic growth. If having your ego deflated by reader

rejection causes you to lose your enthusiasm - and I'm referring to permanent loss; even the best and most successful artists have temporary bouts of discouragement - then you probably don't have enough drive to succeed as a professional. That's not the end of the world, by the way: You don't have to be a careerist or even get paid in order to have fun drawing comics for yourself, your friends, and whomever else you can amuse.

"But maybe you have professional ambitions and can forge ahead in the face of rejection and criticism without getting surly or self-pitying. If so, setting your sights on a professional comics career may be a rational goal. If you can keep your ear cocked for what's valid in other people's criticism of your work and respond creatively to the insights that they have to offer, you'll have the satisfying experience of watching yourself improve steadily. That's a major rush in itself. And over the long haul, if you keep practicing and learning, you'll find other people's praise for your efforts outweighing the putdowns. Meanwhile, you'll be building up your own powers of self-criticism - so that you can spot your own flaws and correct them before they get targeted by caustic smart-ass critics and your own reservoir of self-confidence - for those occasions when you're authentically right and all your critics are wrong.

"Also, never stop examining your reasons for wanting to draw comics. Different people find themselves in this line of work for different reasons. Because you're an individual unlike anyone else, you will need to base your career strategies and your long-term goals on your own individual value system.

"Many people never get around to consciously examining their own value systems: Too often they find themselves trapped in career tracks that may have made them famous but don't truly suit them. For example, there are talented cartoonists who simply get a kick out of drawing superhero fantasies. Put them in charge of *Batman* or *The Fantastic Four* and they'll be in heaven. I, on the other hand, would find drawing a page of superhero art - unless I was spoofing the genre - to be the direst form of torture that the cartooning field could offer, with the possible exception of being an 'in-betweener' for Saturday-morning Hanna-Barbera cartoons. The fact that I would

hate drawing superheroes whereas others love drawing them does not make me a superior life form; it just means that the factors that motivate me to put pen to paper are related to very particular aspects of my personality.

"You're not me; you're you. Spend some time figuring out who that is, and tailor your artistic and career goals accordingly.

"Good luck - and have fun!"

Above and previous page: Artwork from Howard Cruse's Stuck Rubber Baby. *Two pages prior: A panel from* Wendel.

Peter David

Peter David's bio for his widely read Comics Buyer's Guide *column, But I Digress, usually labels him "writer of stuff". That "stuff" includes a number of best-selling* Star Trek *novels and acclaimed runs on* Spider-Man, Wolverine, X-Factor, *and* The Incredible Hulk *at Marvel and* The Atlantis Chronicles *and* Aquaman *at DC.*

Date and place of birth:
September 23rd, 1956; Ft. Meade, Maryland.

Breaking in:
"My pro career in comics began when, in pursuing my 'real' career of sales, I became assistant direct-sales manager at Marvel Comics. Working with then-sales manager Carol Kalish, I focused on getting comics into stores and expanding the direct market. Writing was something that I did on the side. Eventually, just as a lark, I started submitting story premises to editors. One thing led to another and it kind-of snowballed."

Advice to aspiring creators:
"Don't take rejection personally.
"Keep reading, keep writing, and keep your day job."

Right: Peter David, when he gets really, really angry.

Dan Davis

Dan Davis' inking has appeared in Showcase '93 *and* Guy Gardner: Warrior *at DC and* Barb Wire *and* The Thing from Another World *at Dark Horse. He recently inked* The Regulators *for Image.*

Date and place of birth:
September 18th, 1957; Celina, Ohio.

First exposure to comics:
Dan's imagination was captured at an early age by the newspaper strips. "I clipped out *Alley Oop* and made stories, and that started my collection," he recalls. "At nine years old, I received a letter and an original strip from [*Alley Oop* creator] VT Hamlin, and that's what firmed up my desire to work in comics. Later, I bought a *Sgt. Fury* comic book and saw the house ads for *The Fantastic Four* and *Spider-Man*, and I was hooked."

Breaking in:
"I trained myself by copying and creating my own strips," Dan says. After high school, he traveled to New York City to apprentice with veteran artist Dan Adkins, and later returned to Ohio for an undergraduate stint at Bowling Green University. Claiming a BS in visual communications, Dan secured a day job and devoted his spare time to honing his comics skills: "I settled on inking, and sent samples to various editors, including submission editors at Marvel and DC. [Then-DC new-talent coordinator] Neal Pozner called, and he and I kept in touch until he got me my first work at DC."

Advice to aspiring creators:
"My advice to creators is to *create*. Study, practice, and copy to *learn*, but spend the bulk of your time writing and drawing. Only by producing physical work can you tell where you are [in your development].

"Don't be discouraged by criticism or rejection. Learn what you can from it and shake off the negatives. Be flexible, and try everything!"

Suzanne Dechnik

Suzanne Dechnik began her comics career at Now, coloring such series as The Green Hornet, The Twilight Zone, *and* Speed Racer. *More recently, she has colored* Elfquest: Hidden Years, Shards, *and* Blood of Ten Chiefs *for Warp.*

Date and place of birth:
February 14th, 1952; Chicago, Illinois.

First exposure to comics:
"I was but a young pup at some obscure relatives' house and bored out of my mind when I picked up a *Fantastic Four* starring my all-time favorite, Dr. Doom. I was amazed! I started looking for [comics] near my house and became a big fan of Dr. Strange, too."

Breaking in:
"Call it what you will - serendipity, fate, kismet. I had attended the Art Institute, the Chicago Academy of Fine Arts, and the University of Illinois - where I *also* studied art - and Now Comics was looking for a letterer and art assistant for office doo-dah. I answered their ad, and they gave me a blue-line to color and some lettering guidelines. On my second interview, I was told that the other two positions [lettering and art assistance] were filled, but they wanted to hire me as a colorist. I took the job and found that I just loved it."

Advice to aspiring creators:
"Go to art school! So many comics are drawn by people who copied another artist's style, without knowing what it is that the"re doing. It's okay to study your favorite, but learn to draw in your *own* style. Not only is it more soul-enriching, it enables you to be more flexible; you may not get to do comics right away, and [flexibility] would let you do storyboards or something else that might let you keep your hand in it, so to speak.

"Keep trying, and remember that no-one is going to call one fine day and say, 'You're the answer to our prayers! We'll pay you zillions and give you an office with a view! Just please, come work for us!', with clouds of angels singing hosannas and the Earth smelling of roses forevermore.

"Art is *work*. Sometimes it's hard labor, and sometimes you breeze along so effortlessly that it feels like possession, but it's more of the former than you'd like to believe. So you'd better love it."

Sarah Dyer

Sarah Dyer is the editor of Action Girl Comics, *a quarterly anthology of "pro-girl" comics published by Slave Labor Graphics. Sarah has long been active in the world of small-press 'zines, but, through collaborations with partner Evan Dorkin, she can now be found in the mainstream media as well: Among their joint projects are* Kid Blastoff, *serialized in the digest magazine* Disney Adventures; *the scripting of several episodes for the Cartoon Network's* Space Ghost: Coast to Coast; *and short pieces for Dark Horse Comics' wonderful anthology series* Instant Piano.

First exposure to comics/Breaking in:

"My parents were in college when I was a little girl, because my dad got drafted while he was in college and he didn't go back until after I was born. So we grew up surrounded by my parents' college friends' comics. I don't remember it really clearly, but they would all dump their collections on us, so I know that we were reading a lot of late-'60s comics, *Dr. Strange* and stuff. We were reading all the wacky Marvel books as kids; we didn't know *what* they were.

"Like most people, I stopped reading comics when I was around twelve. I was working at the college newspaper a few years ago, and someone I worked with [also] worked at a comics shop, and he kept giving me the books that he didn't want anymore. He gave me some *Love and Rockets* graphic novels and a couple of different things, and some I liked and some I didn't, but I started picking up comics again *then*.

"I don't know how I really started *doing* comics. I got a degree in art, and I've always drawn, [but] I'd never thought to draw in that kind of a format. It just sort-of *happened*. There wasn't any conscious decision, like 'I guess I'll do comics now.'"

Advice to aspiring creators:

"I would say that the most important thing is that people really should stay in

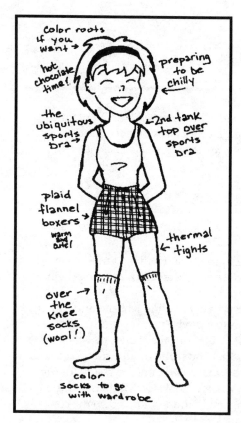

Color roots if you want →

preparing to be chilly ←

hot chocolate time!

the ubiquitous sports bra →

← 2nd tank top over sports bra

plaid flannel boxers →
warm and cute!

thermal ← tights

over → the knee socks (wool!)

color socks to go with wardrobe

minicomics until they're ready. People in minicomics and 'zines, some of them are getting circulations as high or higher than the lower-selling so-called 'professionally' produced books. I think that it's really important that people remember that that's a viable alternative, and it's *much* cheaper and *much* less risky, and you don't have to deal with the distributors and the retailer system. And its a good way to get a lot of feedback on your work.

"I think that if someone has an idea and plunges into spending the money on a four-color cover and getting it listed [in the direct-market distributors' catalogs] and everything, I think that they're going to be really disappointed if it doesn't do well. And I've seen plenty of first issues coming from people who really were not ready to do a professional-level book, and they never got a second issue out. I would also suggest trying to get exposure, get into anthologies, get into print wherever you can, so that people see your work."

Above: Sarah Dyer presents a paper doll for the '90s. Previous page: Jennifer Sorenson's Gwen *from Sarah's* Action Girl Comics.

Steve Erwin

Steve Erwin's artwork has appeared in First's Grimjack *and DC's* Vigilante, Checkmate!, Deathstroke, *and* Gunfire. *Taking a break from the guys-with-guns genre, Steve penciled the DC comics adaptation of William Shatner's first Star Trek novel,* Ashes of Eden.

Date and place of birth:
January 16th, 1960; Tulsa, Oklahoma.

First exposure to comics:
"My parents brought comics home from the store all the time, as varied as you can imagine, from *Superman* to *Archie*. I don't recall buying them myself until I was nine years old or so.

"The earliest story that I remember actually reading was the Superman story where Superman raced the Flash to see who was the fastest. The art impressed me more than the story itself. On the other hand, the story that stands out *most* is a Spider-Man story that ends with Spidey trapped under a huge piece of machinery after a battle, the mass being too heavy for him to budge, and water pouring in everywhere. Cool stuff! But I hated the continued storyline. I was very young, and I didn't quite grasp the concept of monthly shipping schedules of comics.

"My uncle collected early Marvel comics, like *Daredevil* and *The Fantastic Four*. He gave me most of his collection - and I use the term loosely, as the comics were just ones that he hadn't thrown away - for my birthday; I think that I had turned twelve or thirteen. The *FF* stories blew me away, especially the Black Panther story set in Wakanda, but I really didn't 'get' Jack Kirby's style back then. … My opinion was that Marvel's comics looked bad but had cool stories, and DC's comics looked great but were silly. Quite a paradox to a very young mind.

"My biggest exposure to comics in any meaningful context was actually by way of Saturday-morning cartoons, especially *Space Ghost*, *The Herculoids*, and other Hanna-Barbera superhero shows, as well as *Spider-Man* and those really bad *Marvel Superheroes* cartoons, where the art was actually taken from the comics panels. Oh, and don't forget *Jonny Quest!*"

Breaking in:
"I was bored with my job, basically. I was working for petroleum companies' art and drafting departments, doing everything from making

geology slides to spotting gas and oil wells on contour maps. At the time, my wife was editing a *Dr. Who* fanzine to which I occasionally contributed spot illustrations for stories. When I tried to contribute a comics-style story, I discovered how hard it was to actually *draw* comics. I also discovered how much fun it could be!

"When a comics convention opened in my area, Houston at the time, I decided to take my incomplete *Dr. Who* story with me for a critique from the pros. Mike Grell and Joe Staton were there, along with Rick Obadiah, promoting the launch of the First Comics line of books - Grell was talking up his *Jon Sable, Freelance* title; Staton was the art director. They gave me a good review: I wasn't yet 'hirable', but I had potential. They were very forthright with my shortcomings and instructed me in what to work on. They were also kind enough to tell me what I was doing *right*.

"For the next couple of years, I reworked my pages, drew new ones, and went to more conventions for portfolio reviews. Finally, after winning a *Marvel Try-Out Book* contest, which got my work published in [Marvel's in-house fan magazine] *Marvel Age* and brought me a job offer from a would-be independent publisher, I felt as though I was close to going pro. When my wife accepted a job offer near Dallas, she gave me a chance: After we relocated, I could stay home and build a true comics portfolio and try to get into comics. She felt that I should have the opportunity to find out if I *could* be good enough, rather than spend a lifetime wondering. I will always love her for that thoughtfulness.

"I sent my samples to Marvel, DC, First, and Eclipse. I heard back from First in less than two weeks with an offer for a tryout - a

Munden's Bar story in *Grimjack*. That led to penciling a second and third installment, inking the first, and a possible inking position with the artist on the book. I eventually drew some issues of *Shatter*, then moved on to a Texas-based publisher, which soon went out of business. My experience and contacts at First landed me a position at DC - penciling *Vigilante*, then *Checkmate!* - which has led to steady work ever since."

Advice to aspiring creators:

"Depending on what you want to do - create your own material or work on existing titles - the 'road to success' has different signposts. If you want to create your own title or characters, your best bet is to approach an independent publisher with your material ready to go, or to self-publish. If you just want to draw comics, like I did, especially some of your favorite characters from your fan reading, you have to get hired by the right people - and that simply requires you to prove to the right people that you can do the job.

"Once you get an assignment, *get it in on time*. The editor assumes that your pristine samples are the result of long hours spent getting them to look as perfect as possible to show; he also assumes that your 'real' work will look slightly less impressive when you're under the deadline gun. So put your best efforts into making your deadline with pages that are less than perfect, rather than perfect pages that are weeks late. The editor will forgive the art problems and even help you to fix them, but he is primarily concerned with getting the work on time.

"Most importantly, if you *really* want to create comics, and you *really* believe that you might be good enough, *try*. If you fail, if you're not good enough, it's best that you know it, rather than wonder for the rest of your life, 'Could I have?'"

Previous page: Steve Erwin's rendition of Gunfire.

Michael Eury

Michael Eury edited The Legion of Super-Heroes *and* Eclipso: The Darkness Within *for DC and* Ghost, The Mask, *and* Batman vs. Predator II *for Dark Horse. His writing credits include Dark Horse's* Hero Zero *and an upcoming story arc in the new* Adventures of the Mask.

Date and place of birth:
September 28th, 1957; Concord, North Carolina.

First exposure to comics:
"My parents, having read comics when they were kids, gave me comic books - Disney, Gold Key, Harvey - at a pre-school age to encourage me to learn to read. Then, when in the third grade, I was exposed to superheroes via Adam West's *Batman* series. It was an epiphany for me."

Breaking in:
"After rolling with the punches of rejection after rejection of story proposals, I was lucky enough to have 'over-the-transom' article pitches sell, almost simultaneously, to the now-defunct *Marvel Age* and *Amazing Heroes*; Jim Salicrup and Mark Waid, the editors of each book, respectively, then assigned me more work, which grew into writing short stories, and then into editing."

Advice to aspiring creators:
• "Focus. Don't try to be an expert writer/artist/colorist on day one. Pick a craft and get good at it, *then* branch out.
• "Meet your deadlines. You can be the most talented visionary out there, but *reliability* and *regularity* help hone your skills and develop an audience.
• "Never forget that ther''s always room for improvement with your work."

Left: The Mask, penciled by Doug Mahnke and inked by Keith Williams.

Matt Feazell

Matt Feazell's work has delighted scores of jaded comics fans the world over. A heaping helping of his diverse minicomics output was collected last summer by Caliber Press in the trade paperback Ert!, *and such seminal works as* The Death of Antisocialman *(still in progress) and* Understanding Minicomics *are currently in stock at Matt's own Not Available Comics. For the snobbish, Matt's "regular-size" comics work includes the* Zot in Dimension 10-1/2 *series in Eclipse's* Zot! *and a story in First's* Munden's Bar Annual.

Date and place of birth:
May 11th, 1955; Ames, Iowa.

First exposure to comics:

Matt recalls Gold Key mystery comics, *Mad Magazine*, DC war books like *Sgt. Rock* and *Enemy Ace*, and *Peanuts* paperbacks from his childhood, but says that comic books really didn't make much of an impression on him until he was in junior high school, when he and a friend began collecting Marvel's *Fantastic Four*.

"TV and movie animation made a bigger impression on me," he recalls. "Disney's *101 Dalmatians* was the first movie that I ever saw in a theatre and I was totally enthralled by it. I watched a lot of Saturday-morning and after-school cartoons, which I think accounts for my tendency to draw comics in a grid of identically sized panels - kind-of like a television screen. My *earliest* memory of watching cartoons on TV is watching a Max Fleischer *Popeye* cartoon - I must have been five at the time - and seeing if I could project my voice into the cartoon by shouting into the TV's speaker. Later on, I was a big fan of *Rocky and Bullwinkle* and all the other Jay Ward cartoons."

Breaking in:
"I started drawing stick-figure comics in my school notebooks when I was thirteen, and I kept it up all through junior high school and into senior high school. Exposure to Marvel comics inspired me to try drawing 'full-figure'-style.

"Through college and the first couple of years after, my work appeared in fanzines and apas as I tried to polish a Marvel- or *Heavy Metal*-influenced professional-art style, but I found that I was spending most of my drawing time producing portfolio samples that I hoped would impress an editor and get me a job and very little time actually drawing comics that interested me.

"Along about three years out of college, I was working in a used-record store, listening to lots of punk rock and new-wave music. I was inspired by an Elvis Costello song to get back to basics and try drawing comics again like I did when I first started back in junior high and drew just for the love of drawing and telling a story and not to impress a client or an editor in hopes that they would give me a job. I took a morose-looking 'un-smiley' face that had been lurking in the margins of my sketchbook, called him the Amazing Cynicalman, and drew a quick story on the back of a record-store handout.

"I posted the first few *Cynicalman* adventures on telephone poles and vacant buildings near my job and apartment and also mailed some to friends and fanzine pals. In about three weeks I got a minicomic in the mail - Walt Roger's *Just Another Eight-Page Wonder*. It inspired me to try *Cynicalman* as an eight-page minicomic. Suddenly, I was having fun drawing comics again.

"I discovered that total strangers would pay twenty-five cents for a stick-figure minicomic. By selling and giving away my minicomics at conventions, to comics shops, and through the mail, I built a network of associations with other artists and through that eventually came to the notice of comic-book editors and publishers. …

"Jay Kennedy saw my self-published comics advertised in *Comics Buyer's Guide* in 1980. He sent for them, wrote back a letter of praise, and suggested that I send them to Jay Kinney, who was writing a comics-review column in *Heavy Metal*. One of the comics that I sent to Kinney was *Invasion of Earth*, which had a punk rock-influenced theme of political anarchy; a few months later called me to ask if I wanted to contribute to an issue of *Anarchy Comics* that he was editing. My story appeared in *Anarchy Comics* #3.

"One of my minicomic correspondents turned out to be Scott

McCloud, the creator of *Zot!*. When *Zot!* went on hiatus after the first ten issues, Scott wanted to try some other projects, one of which was a *Zot!* minicomic. He sent me the script and breakdowns for a Zot-Cynicalman team-up that became the *Zot!* #10-1/2 minicomic which led to *Giant-Size Mini-Comics*, the *Dimension 10-1/2* feature in the new *Zot!* series, and the [regular-format] *Cynicalman* comic book, all published by Eclipse.

"So the irony of it all is that I managed to break into comics with a style and a character that was inspired by a desire *not* to break into comics. By doing the exact opposite of what the accepted wisdom says that one should do to break into comics, I got my chance. Instead of submitting portfolios and asking an editor to hire me to draw comics, I just started drawing the comics that I wanted to draw and telling stories that amused myself.

"Of course, I still work at a newspaper making display ads on a computer, so this *may* not qualify as a story about how to break into comics. I'm having a great time, though."

Advice to aspiring creators:

"Comics is a shrinking field. There are fewer readers of mainstream comics all the time. The big companies make more money off of merchandising their characters than on sales of the books now. I see the actual writing and drawing of comics becoming more of a folk art in coming years.

"The five-cent copy shop has changed *everything*. Now, with the easy availability of high-speed photocopiers and home computers, the art of comics-making is moving out of the hands of high-stakes publishers and into the hands of common people with something to say and the itch to create."

Above: A scene from Zot in Dimension 10-1/2, *written by E. Yarber and drawn by Matt Feazell. Previous page: A sequence from Matt's* Understanding Minicomics. *Before that, even: The amazing Cynicalman.*

Mary Fleener

Mary Fleener is the creator of Slutburger, *published by Drawn and Quarterly. Her work has also appeared in numerous comics anthologies and in such diverse publications as* Entertainment Weekly, The Village Voice, *and* Hustler.

Date and place of birth:
September 14th, 1951; Los Angeles, California.

First exposure to comics:
"The *LA Times* and *LA Herald-Examiner* Sunday comic sections fascinated me," Mary recalls. "Then, in the fourth grade, my brother showed me a *Mad* magazine, which I found disturbing, alien, and utterly addictive.

"In 1969, I saw my first issue of *Zap Comix* and fantasized about doing underground comics. In 1985, after reading an article that Matt Groening wrote in *LA Weekly* about 'the new comics', I finally decided to."

Breaking in:
"I started doing minicomics, then edited a digest-size anthology, *Chicken Slacks*, illustrating music lyrics - rock 'n' roll, blues, etc. - and met lots of people. I sent books to my 'idols' and just got to know as many artists as possible. I asked a lot of questions, and my first comics art was published in the *The Couch Potato Newsletter*, edited by one of my heroes, Robert Armstrong. Then I went for the anthologies, like *Weirdo* and *Wimmens*, where chances of getting published were better than [those of] landing a book deal. I was *always focused*, however, towards doing underground or alternative subject matter - *no* superheroes!"

Advice to aspiring creators:
- "Don't swipe. There will always be someone with a good eye and good memory who will bust you!
- "Learning cartooning and getting published is like learning a musical instrument. It will take some years for your grand plan to gel.
- "Never take rejection personally. Instead, go back to square one and use that anger and resolve to create an even *greater masterpiece*. They'll all come around sooner or later!"

Carl Gafford

Carl Gafford is a veteran of DC Comics' production department and was a freelance colorist from for more than fifteen years, lending his palette to such DC series as The Flash, Legion of Super-Heroes, *and* Justice League of America. *He was the production manager at Disney Comics, where he edited the* Aladdin *mini-series, and currently holds the same position at Topps Comics, for which he colors a variety of titles. Short stories written and drawn by Carl have appeared in* Wildlife, Furrlough, *and* Shanda the Panda, *published by Antarctic Press.*

Date and place of birth:
November 23rd, 1952; Attleboro, Massachusetts.

First exposure to comics:
Carl's first exposure to comics was the Silver-Age Flash's final appearance in *Showcase* - #14, dated March of 1958. "Impressed with it," he says, "I promptly told my grandmother - who'd bought the book for me - to get me 'more'. After all, there was a new Superman-related title every week... Why not the same for Flash? I was ahead of myself: Now there are weekly titles for Spider-Man, X-Men, the Justice League, etc...."

Breaking in:
"In the summer of 1972, I drew a 'safe' draft-lottery number that ensured that I'd stay out of the draft until Ho Chi Minh and Jane Fonda hoisted the Viet Cong colors at Disneyland. Working full-time at a newspaper doing typesetting, paste-ups, and proofreading wasn't bringing in the bucks, so I camped out on Tony Isabella's couch in January of 1973 and took my portfolio around.

"My portfolio was a bust, but my resumé listed paste-up and production experience, so Sol Harrison at DC gave me a proofreading test and then asked me to come back two days later for a second test. I found out why that night. While waiting to see Sol, I spent some time talking to Paul Levitz. Paul and I had known each other in fandom - I helped him man the fandom table in 1972 at the July Comicon, where he sold copies of my fanzine, *Minotaur*. After I left, Sol grilled Paul on what he knew about me, and he, in turn, told me that night at his place what they asked about me, so that I was prepared with the right answers for their questions on my second interview. The result: I was hired as assistant proofreader starting in March of 1973.

"I was promoted to assistant production manager in August of 1974, left staff in September of 1976, returned five years later to my proofreader job, and was soon promoted to Len Wein's assistant editor, a position that I left in 1982. You just don't get jobs like that to quit any more."

Advice to aspiring creators:

"Nothing is more important than having Real World Experience. My first job came as a result of real experience at a newspaper, doing typesetting and paste-ups in the ad department.

"If you're an artist, learn the rules of real art: Anatomy, perspective, how clothes fold, how a person sits in a chair or in a car. If you can really draw, you can learn to draw comics - but it's not a given the other way around.

"If you're a writer, learn to *write* first, *then* learn to write comics. Learn to spell, learn to write dialogue that sounds individualistic to each speaker, learn how to construct a plot.

"There's nothing wrong with being a writer or an artist who does comics, but there's a *lot* wrong if you're a writer or an artist who can *only* do comics."

Previous page: A "furry" tribute to horror comics from the last issue of Wild Life, *courtesy Carl Gafford*

Rick Geary

Rick Geary's comics and illustrated stories have appeared in National Lampoon, Heavy Metal, *and* Dark Horse Comics. *A 1995 National Cartoonists Society awardwinner, Rick is the writer and artist of three* Classics Illustrated *adaptations - Great Expectations, Wuthering Heights, and The Invisible Man - for First , of* A Treasury of Victorian Murder *for NBM, and of* The Mask's Summer Vacation *for Dark Horse.*

Date and place of birth:
February 25th, 1946; Kansas City, Missouri.

First exposure to comics:
"I was never a real comics fan or collector," Rick says, "but as a young kid I truly loved Carl Barks' Uncle Scrooge stories. Later on, I discovered *Mad Magazine*. I *never* imagined that I would someday make a living in the field."

Breaking in:
"In the '70s, I worked as a cartoonist/illustrator for weekly papers in Wichita, Kansas, and San Diego, California. My first comics story was published - through my pal Scott Shaw - in *Fear and Laughter*, an anthology derived from the exploits of Hunter S. Thompson and published in 1977 by Kitchen Sink. But I guess that I really 'broke in' when David Scroggy showed my self-published minibooks to Shary Flenniken at *National Lampoon* in 1979, and I thus became a regular contributor."

Advice to aspiring creators:
- "You must *love* to draw.
- "Show your work to as *many* people as will look at it.
- "If no-one will publish you, publish yourself."

Nat Gertler

Nat Gertler has written for Warp Graphics' Elfquest: New Blood, *Milestone Media's* Blood Syndicate, *Entity Comics'* Zen: Intergalactic Ninja, *and a host of other comic-book series. His articles have appeared in* Comics Buyer's Guide, Wizard: The Guide to Comics, *and* Comics Career Newsletter.

Date and place of birth:
   April 30th, 1965; Our Lady of Lourdes Hospital, Camden, New Jersey.

First exposure to comics:
   "I was reading *Richie Rich* and *Little Archie* as far back as I can recall. Then the price of *Little Archie* went up a nickel, and I became a *Richie Rich*-only guy. It wasn't until college that I got a major exposure to superheroes, but that turned me into an adventure-comics addict."

Breaking in:
   "I was always a writer, but I never really thought about writing comics until I sat next to *Marvel Two-in-One* penciler Ron Wilson on a bus, and suddenly realized that there were people out there who actually made the things! Over the next few years, I submitted plots to Marvel on a couple of occasions, to no avail.
   "Eventually, I decided to take the self-publishing route, but rather than do it with an original creation, I wanted to license *Speed Racer.* A friend of mine who was in the licensing business set on the arduous task of establishing who held the rights. The very day that he found the owner, Now Comics announced that *it* had licensed the rights, so those hopes were dashed.
   "A short while later, [the people at] Now announced that they needed to

replace their writer on that project, and I sent a copy of what I had wanted to do with the series as a sample. By the time they got [the submission], they already had a new regular writer, but they were impressed with my plans and had me turn them into the story that ran in *Speed Racer* #21-22. The story took about a year and a half to see print, by which time I had two other pieces of comics work published.

"[There was] a long, dry spell, and then the work started to come in spurts. After a few years of this, I knew that I had to take a *serious* stab. With the money that I had saved from the day job, computer programming, I started trying to write full-time. I went through the savings and into debt, but the turnaround for the writing career came when I used my comics-writing experience to get [work on] a heavily illustrated computer book, *Computers Illustrated*. The money from that has carried me over until now, when suddenly I find that I may have more comics-writing projects than I have time for."

Advice to aspiring creators:

"First, check your reason for trying to break into comics. If it's just 'I love comics', that's a great reason for reading them, but that's not enough to make them your living. If it's 'I really want to work in the field of comics', realize that most of the jobs in the field are not in writing or drawing, but in publishing, distributing, and selling these comics, and your energies may be better expended in those directions. And if all you want to do is create your own special stories in this unique medium, there's no reason that that has to be a *profession*; there can be great creative fulfillment in creating your own photocopied comics for local distribution, without most of the heart-aches of working in the industry.

"But if you decide to go for the big prize, figure out what the big prize *is* for you. Is it drawing your favorite superhero? Is it doing all of the creative chores on your own autobiographical series? Is it having hordes of beauti-ful groupies? Then, as you try to take the next step towards breaking in - and 'breaking in' is a process; it isn't just making one sale that separates those who haven't made it from those who have - check that step and make sure that it gets you closer to your prize. That doesn't mean that you should never do things that don't [get you closer] - sometimes you may get a project that doesn't do anything but help put food on your table, and that can be important; sometimes a project doesn't build toward that prize, but it's fun, and that can be worthwhile. Watch out, though: It's easy to end up getting too distracted by trying to get *any* work in the field, wasting a lot of time and building a lot of bad habits that pull you away from your prize."

Previous page: A Wendy Pini pencil sketch from Elfquest's *original run.*

Tom Gill

Tom Gill drew The Lone Ranger *for Dell and Gold Key for twenty years, during which time his artwork also graced the pages of such* Ranger *spinoffs as* Tonto *and* Hi-Yo, Silver *and numerous other Western and romance titles for Gold Key, Harvey, Timely, and DC. Tom has illustrated several children's books, has chaired the National Cartoonists Society, and was a founding faculty member of New York's Cartoonists and Illustrators School, now the School of Visual Arts, where he still serves as a consultant and instructor.*

Date and place of birth:

June 3rd, 1913; Winnipeg, Canada. (Tom's parents were on a business trip from New York at the time, and he was born a US citizen.)

First exposure to comics/Breaking in:

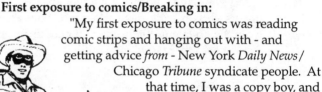

"My first exposure to comics was reading comic strips and hanging out with - and getting advice *from* - New York *Daily News*/ Chicago *Tribune* syndicate people. At that time, I was a copy boy, and I wanted to be a cartoonist. I was there the day Dale Messick sold *Brenda Starr*.

"I did all the maps for *The Daily News* during World War Two. By that time, I had finally gotten into the art department. And to get out of that grind, I created a strip about a cab driver and placed it with *The Herald-Tribune*. In the meantime, the School of Visual Arts was starting up, but at that time we called it the Cartoonists and Illustrators School, C&I. I was an executive for the school almost from the start."

Advice to aspiring creators:

"You have to be driven. You have to emerge from the amateur, the dawdler, the dilettante, into the professional. And that takes a lot of dedication and a lot of hard work. You have to be driven. [The work] has to be the prime motivation in your life.

"You *should* be a rounded person - that follows in any art form. I consider cartooning and writing performing arts.

"Learn things in short spurts: Don't undertake too much and burden yourself. You accomplish your goals sooner that way, and you're encouraged to carry on.

"I don't want to discourage people from going to school; the more help they get, the better off they are. But in my classes, I don't teach people *how to cartoon*. If I did that, I'd be teaching them *my* vision. What I want to do is draw out *their* vision. In today's cartooning field, it's so wide-open, it's so *un*prescribed, that anything goes. No matter what you come up with, you don't have to fear anymore that it isn't the 'right' way. As in fashion, as in music, as in everything, the field is just wide-open.

"Certain talents, certain aptitudes, certain directions are needed to move the world. Even the no-talents are needed. If people are given a talent, it's in them, and it just *bugs* them until they fulfill it."

Previous page: Tom Gill's rendition of the Lone Ranger.

Stan Goldberg

Stan Goldberg has put in more than fifty years at the drawing board, over half of them at Archie Comics. Though a versatile artist, Stan is best known for his work on teenage-humor stories for Archie, Marvel, and DC, and co-penciled the land-mark Archie/Marvel crossover, Archie Meets the Punisher. *He continues to provide covers for nearly half of the Archie line each month.*

Date and place of birth:
May 5th, 1932; New York, New York.

First exposure to comics:
Stan grew up reading *Captain America* and *The Human Torch,* and after art school found himself working for their publisher, Timely - the forerunner of Marvel. "All around me were Carl Burgos, Bill Everett, guys like that who *drew* the comics," he remembers. "So it was really a dream come true."

Breaking in:
"Even as a child, I would make my own picture books," Stan says. "It seemed like it was never enough to do just one picture, and then another that was completely different - I always had to tie in a little story, whether it was humor or adventure stuff, a beginning and a middle and an end. ...

"I studied cartooning the last two years of high school - it was an art school - and we covered all the bases: Gag cartoons, spot illustrations, comics, lettering design. When I went to work at Timely, I went back to the School of Visual Arts and I studied there for another two years. One of the instructors, I remember, was Jerry Robinson; Jerry was working for Timely at that time, and I was working on a lot of his stuff, because I was in the coloring department - I ran the coloring department for many years.

"I went to start at Timely when I'd just turned seventeen; it was 1949 - not 1849, though it seems like it sometimes! My first job up there was in the coloring department, and in the beginning I wasn't even allowed to put the color on the pages; I was just cleaning out the brushes and the jars and mixing flesh color. Finally, they started teaching me how to work, even though I kinda knew all that already. When you get there, there's still a learning process. But after about a year, I was in charge of the coloring department. We were also putting out a lot of horror books, and I was drawing horror stories in *Marvel Tales* and *Tales to Astonish* - this was in the early and mid '50s. I had no idea that I would wind up for the next thirty years doing teenage and romance [comics]. It just happened one day, in the late '50s - and it was probably the second-best thing that ever happened to me. I survived all these years working on that stuff, and enjoying it tremendously. It's more fun doing teenage humor and romance than doing the heavy, heavy stuff. …

"I did the humor books for Marvel - *Millie the Model*, and *Patsy Walker*, and *My Girl Pearl* - and then I did the humor books for DC - *Scooter*, and *Binky's Buddies*, and *Debbie's Dates* . But slowly, Marvel and DC were so concentrated on putting out superheroes that my books were having a big problem, because the writing wasn't that great, and they were concentrating on the superheroes, so that's when I went over to Archie. I knew that someday I'd be knocking on their door, and there I was."

Advice to aspiring creators:

"Getting to work in comics at that early age [after art school] was a great training ground for me. No matter how much time you put in at school, the best experience is getting out there in the field, right next to the guys who are doing it, and doing it with them. If the guys are good enough, and if you're patient enough with them, and if they"e patient enough with *you*, you can't ask for anything better than that.

"Drawing comics - not just Archie comics, but drawing anything - it's a seven-day-a-week job. You must keep your eyes and ears open to whatever's happening around you, because that, in turn, you will use in your pictures. If you can develop your mind like a camera, and remember all of these little things that you see that have interest to you, funny things that happen to you, or passing a building that looks interesting, or people walking down the street - things that you register in your head… If you can do that, work at it, and then sit down at your desk and draw your pictures, all these little things will come out on your page.

"I'm constantly on the look for new talent. If I see young writers and artists who have some ability, I refer them to [Archie editor Victor Gorelick], and there are sample stories that they can work on. In the past few years, we've had about four or five young artists working for us. We put out a lot of material, and we do a lot of commercial books also - companies use our characters on books that they give away; I did a whole series of them for a telephone company in New England, and major stores all over the country, even the FBI. Some months, we can put out fifteen to eighteen titles, including our digest books.

"Victor is always looking at new stuff, or some new artist that he's developing, and he has my advice. Teenage-humor material is not something that people just bang out. It looks quite easy to do, but I feel - and I've heard this talking to many artists, guys who've been around for a long time, like John Romita and John Buscema and Gene Colan - that drawing teenage-humor stories is more difficult than drawing superheroes and adventure stories.

"We're appealing to a different audience, maybe a younger audience, ages eight and nine up to eleven or twelve. We have to be aware of styles of clothes, of hairdos, of the way kids move. I talked to a young artist who had the storytelling down, but then I saw that he had four characters there and it looked like every one of them [looked] just alike. Put four boys and girls together, even though their styles kind-of look alike, and you have to make them a little different - even think of the characters as real people. Archie doesn't walk like Reggie, and Reggie certainly doesn't walk like Jughead, and the girls don't act the same when they're all together. …

"Somebody said to me, 'You draw the same characters year after year. You could probably do it with your eyes closed.' And I said, 'If I could draw these characters with my eyes closed, I would put my pencil down and I would never draw again, because that would bore me to death.' I keep my eyes wide open."

Previous page: Archie and his two best gals, Betty and Veronica, as rendered by Stan Goldberg.

Steve Hauk

Steve Hauk is a longtime contributing cartoonist to Comics Buyer's Guide.
His comic-book work includes the Fish Police *mini-series* Fish Shticks *for Apple
Comics, various logos and spot illustrations for Caliber Press, and inks on* Barbie
Fashion *for Marvel Comics.*

Date and place of birth:
August 4th, 1954; Washington, DC.

First exposure to comics:
"I would get comics sometimes as little rewards when I was a kid," Steve
recalls. "My interest picked up when the local 7-11 put in a spinner rack
filled with stuff like Jim Steranko's *Nick Fury*, Jack Kirby's *Fantastic Four*,
Herb Trimpe's *Hulk*, and Gene Colan's *Daredevil*."

Breaking in:
"I started making comics to entertain myself," Steve says. "Then I got
small jobs doing flyers, business-card logos, murals, local-theatre program
covers, and fanzines."

Steve's connections from fan activity served him well. Some time ago,
when reading something from Apple Comics, he noticed that the publisher

was an old acquaintance - "someone
whom I had done fanzine work for
twenty years ago," he says. After
making the connection, Steve mailed
in some current samples of his work.

"As it happened, [Apple] was
looking for an artist to draw a new
series of *Fish Police* comics with creator
Steve Moncuse writing, so I produced
model sheets of the main characters
and sent them in. I got the job because
I drew the characters *in my style*,
unlike the other artists who tried out
attempting to imitate Steve Moncuse's
drawings. Unfortunately, it's often the
opposite case when working for the
big companies, who look for stylistic

clones of popular comic-book artists."

Advice to aspiring creators:

• "Show your best work to artists at conventions to get feedback. These folks can't hire you, but they can comment on your work and suggest corrections or praise strengths.

• "Send samples to companies using characters that they *publish* - pictures of Archie and Jughead won't get you work with DC Comics.

• "Small jobs beget larger, more important jobs, and unless you're asleep at the wheel each experience should develop your talent, technique, and discipline."

• "Your samples are your audition; make it count. Let each rejection letter only reaffirm your resolve to do better."

Above and previous page: A sample of Steve Hauk's Comic Shopping *strip.*

Phillip Hester

Phillip Hester has progressed from drawing backup stories in First Comics'
Badger *and* Nexus *to penciling* Swamp Thing *and the recent* Argus *mini-series
for DC. His past output also includes short stories in Caliber's* Negative Burn,
Spiderbaby's Taboo, *and Dark Horse's* Underground.

Date and place of birth:
August 27th, 1966; Cedar Rapids, Iowa.

First exposure to comics:
"Those cheesy department-store three-packs. It was the time of *The
Micronauts, Devil Dinosaur,* and *Rom.* I was in love."

Breaking in:
"I went to art school and began working for tiny, non-paying companies
at nineteen. It's been a slow but always forward progression since then."

Advice to aspiring creators:
Phillip offers the following advice, equally practical and Zen.

• "No-one will break you into comics; *you* will have to do that. It's your
job to take whatever negative emotions that come from rejection and
channel them into creativity. I know a lot of very talented people who
never got over their first portfolio review. So take that anger, resentment,
depression, *whatever* and turn it into a sort of righteous burn.

• "Unless an editor has a background in the creative aspect of comics,
take what he or she has to say with a grain of salt.

• "If an editor tears you apart, he's the one to listen to. If you can win
him over, you can get the rest.

• "If more than two editors tell you something, then it's probably true.

• "When editors say, 'Take life drawing,' they usually don't mean it.
Any decent life-drawing class teaches you how to make a sensitive, unique
interpretation of the model in front of you, not how to draw stomach
muscles right every time. If you want anatomy like Gil Kane or Burne
Hogarth or Andrew Loomis you're going to have to look at their work and
learn from it.

• "Wanting to do comics means *doing* them, whether that's a prestige-
format graphic novel from a huge company or drawing on grocery bags
and stapling them together in your basement."

Bob Ingersoll

Bob Ingersoll has written issues of Star Trek, Star Trek: The Next Generation, *and* Vigilante *for DC,* Moon Knight *for Marvel,* Tales of the Green Hornet *for Now, and* Sentry, Hero Alliance, Lost in Space, *and* Quantum Leap *for Innovation. His Mickey Mouse and Donald Duck stories for Egmont, publisher of fine Disney comics abroad, have appeared in many languages that Bob can't read. A public defender in his secret identity, he also writes long-running column* The Law is a Ass *for Comics Buyer's Guide.*

Date and place of birth:
    October 13th, 1952; Cleveland, Ohio.

First exposure to comics:
    "My first exposure to comics probably came from Lesher's Shoe Store in Shaker Heights," Bob recalls. "The store used to buy comics in bulk and give them out free to kids who bought shoes there. I started reading them back then, liked them, and haven't stopped yet."

Breaking in:
    Don't remind Bob that he made his first professional sale more than twenty years ago. "Back in 1975, Tony Isabella told Paul Kupperberg that Charlton was looking for scripts for its horror/mystery comics. I went to college with a friend of Paul's, who passed the information on to me. I submitted some plots to Charlton through the mail, and Charlton bought them."

Some years later, when, now out of law school and a good friend of Isabella's, Bob became a regular contributor to *Comics Buyer's Guide.* "For months, Tony had been suggesting to me that I should write an article about the law and comics. I kept ignoring him, because I figured that no-one would want to read such a thing. Then, one day shortly after Don and Maggie [Thomspon] became editors of *CBG*, Tony came to me and told me that Don and Maggie wanted the article.

"'What article?' I asked him.

"'The article on law and comics,' he answered.

"When I politely pointed out that I had never pitched the article to them, Tony told me that he'd pitched it *for* me, without my knowledge, because he knew that *I* would never get around to it. But when I started thinking about the article, I realized that it would be monstrously large and came up with the idea of the column, which Don and Maggie also bought. The rest is history." Bob made *The Law is a Ass* a recurring feature, and offered free legal advice to any comics writer needing it for a story; thankfully for his column, not many took him up on the offer - but some more scripting assignments followed.

Advice to aspiring creators:

"If you're really serious, keep trying. It's a very competitive and difficult market to crack, made even more competitive and difficult, at present, by the current market conditions.

"I'm sure that many of the other creators in this book have already given all the advice that I could give, but there is one point that I feel must be made. If no-one else has made it, it needs to be heard. If someone else has said it already, it bears repeating:

"Don't give up your day job!

"The market is in a state of flux, with new companes going into and out of business almost every month. The fact that you've landed a gig with some publisher doesn't mean that your career is now fully launched. Accept the gigs, do them, but *keep your day job*. Wait to see how things are working out for you. If, after a sufficient period of time, it appears that you will be able to get enough work to make a full-time career out of comics, by all means do so - and tell me how you did it. But until then, your financial well-being really requires you to *keep your day job*."

What Bob's trying to say here is…

Previous page: Bob Ingersoll's best Halloween costume yet.

Tony Isabella

Tony Isabella, America's most beloved comic-book writer and columnist according to the independent research firm of Tony Isabella, has been working in the comics field for over two decades as a retailer, a distributor, a journalist, a lecturer, a consultant, and a show promoter. The creator of DC Comics' Black Lightning, *Tony's writing and/or editing credits range from Marvel's* The Amazing Spider-Man *to DC's* Young Love. *Currently, while developing new comic-book properties, he writes the weekly column* Tony's Tips *for* Comics Buyer's Guide *and the monthly column* The Write Stuff *for* Comics Pro Magazine.

Date and place of birth:
December 22nd, 1951; Cleveland, Ohio.

First exposure to comics:
"When I was three years old, my mother used to read comic books and 'real' books to me. Both made a lasting impression, but I learned to read from the comics by the time I was four." Tony doesn't remember his very first comic book, but he narrows it down to one of three - *Red Mask, Casper,* or *Fighting American.*

Breaking in:
"I started writing for comics fanzines in my teens. I also wrote to my favorites editors and writers, several of whom - Murray Boltinoff, Steve Englehart, and Roy Thomas, among others - were kind enough to write back. I wrote hundreds of articles and stories for fanzines and joined several comics apas.

"Since breaking into comics writing was such a long shot, I went to work for *The (Cleveland) Plain Dealer*. Any aspirations that I had toward continuing my budding career as a real-life Clark Kent were dashed when I realized what a lousy paper it was.

"My ticket out came when we went on strike. The *PD* publisher called his friend, the mayor of Cleveland, and asked him to do something about the picket lines in front of his building. The next thing I knew, our picket line was being charged by mounted policemen. I was knocked down by an overweight copy editor fleeing for his life. My face pressed to the sidewalk, I got to see a view of a horse's hoof from an unnatural angle. I still have nightmares about it.

"That evening, I phoned Roy Thomas and asked if anyone at Marvel had a job for me. Fortunately, they needed someone who knew their old comics to package reprints for Great Britain. Two weeks later, I was in New York City adding 'u' to 'color' and stuff like that."

Advice to aspiring creators:
"Write, write, write. Draw, draw, draw. Show what you've drawn and what you've written to anyone who will look it. Get it published, even if it's in a fanzine. Listen to criticism, but don't assume that everybody is giving you good advice.

"As you work towards a career in comics, make sure that you *always* have something to fall back on. There are no guarantees in the comics industry; a creator needs something to see him or her through the dry spells.

"You should also read and study Lurene Haines' *Getting into the Business of Comics*, perhaps the best book ever written on the subject.

"Most importantly, be yourself. The comics art form needs new and unique voices."

Previous page: Intense Eddy Newell artwork of Tony Isabella's creation Black Lightning.

Gerard Jones

Gerard Jones is one of mainstream comics' most prolific writers. His solo credits include Hulk 2099 *and* Wonder Man *for Marvel,* Break-Thru *and* UltraForce *for Malibu's Ultraverse line, and* El Diablo, Justice League International, *and* The Shadow Strikes! *for DC. With longtime collaborator Will Jacobs, he created and wrote* The Trouble with Girls *and various spinoffs for a number of publishers, and he has scripted translations of Japanese cartoonist Rumiko Takahashi's* Ranma 1/2, Maison Ikkoku, *and* Lum: Urusei Yatsura *for Viz.*

Date and place of birth:
July 10th, 1957; Cutbank, Montana.

First exposure to comics:
"My English-teacher mother, believing that comics were harmful garbage, pretty successfully kept me away from the things, except for the occasional Superman or Batman snuck in from neighborhood friends - a couple of coverless *Detective Comics* from the early '60s were among my hidden treasures, and still haunt me - or the stacks of Archies left by a female cousin at my uncle's house. When I was thirteen, however, one of my mother's brighter students convinced her that Marvel comics had some sort of quasi-literary worth - by quoting from a Stan Lee *Silver Surfer*, I think - and she encouraged me to borrow some from him.

"The floodgates were opened. From ages thirteen to fifteen, I spent all of my allowance on back issues, when most of the Marvel backlog was available at five-for-a-dollar and *Fantastic Four* #1 was a nigh-unattainable twenty bucks; lived and breathed Marvel superheroes, with a few choice DCs; and aspired someday to work in comics. Then I discovered, no, not 'girls and cars' as the comics-industry cliché would have it, but bookish-geek-fodder like *Crime and Punishment* and *Paradise Lost*, and I put away all thoughts of comics.

"In my early twenties, working at a used-book store where I could pick up recent back issues for seven cents apiece, I found my curiosity for comics reawakening. There I also met Will Jacobs, who had been a rabid DC boy in the '60s, and who introduced me to the wonders of the Infantino *Flash* and the Kane *Green Lantern*. Suddenly I was a collector again, but with hardly any thoughts of working in the business, until fate came calling..."

Breaking in:

"['Breaking in'] is an odd phrase to use in my case, with its implications of flinging oneself again and again at a locked door until it finally cracks under the sheer energy and persistence of one's blows and one finds oneself at last in the perfumed chamber of that too-desired and shielded object of love. In my case, 'stumbled in' is more like it.

"After Will and I sold our humor book, *The Beaver Papers,* to Crown Publishers, we were casting around for a quick follow-up to sell before our editor lost interest in us, and we decided to do a nostalgic romp through the comics of our respective childhoods. Somehow in the writing of it, *The Comic-Book Heroes* also became a critical look at the comics of the present, as of 1984, in the course of which we interviewed and met a number of people involved in the comics biz. Among these were Dave Olbrich and Tom Mason, then with Fantagraphics, and their pal Mike Valerio. When Dave and Tom launched the Malibu line, Mike

suggested that we contact them if we had any comic-book ideas that we wanted to write. We didn't, particularly, except for an abortive humor novel called *The Trouble with Girls* that we thought might come back to life in a new medium. We bounced the idea off of them, they liked it, and suddenly there we were with a monthly comic book of our own.

"Smelling a way to make a living as a writer, and excited by the prospect of playing with adventure characters in my own sandbox, I then started pursuing opportunities more aggressively, while Will focused on his novels and his plans to open a used-book store of his own. Among other contacts that we'd made was Mark Waid, who as a neophyte assistant editor at DC went around advertising me to other editors as a promising writer; this, combined with my Malibu work, soon resulted in Brian Augustyn offering me the *El Diablo* job, which led to one gig after another at DC. And there was Carl Potts, who bought a couple of never-published plots from me for

Amazing High Adventures and spoke well of me at Marvel, which I'm sure helped induce people there to work with me."

Advice to aspiring creators:
"When asked what advice I'd give to a newcomer trying to 'break in', I usually only flap my mouth foolishly. About all that I can offer - and I think that it's good advice - is to 'network'. Find other promising writers and artists and would-be editors and just hang around with them, talking comics a lot, trying different projects with them - minicomics, self-publishing, illustrated proposals for series. Don't waste your time sending plot summaries for established heroes to overworked editors who already have lists of writers whom they want to work with. Don't count on anyone reading that long proposal for a neat new mini-series, not unless you have a good artist attached. Just become part of the community of comics and, somehow or other, opportunities will present themselves… I *think*. I mean, it worked for *me*, but I was never *trying* to make it work. If you push it, the magic may not happen.

"The only fairly predictable route in this business, if you're willing to move to New York and live on nothing for years, is to become an intern or low-level employee at Marvel or DC and haunt the halls sniffing for opportunities, climbing the ladder, nagging editors into giving you a chance. It's amazing how many people now prominent in the business started that way. If nothing else, it'll teach you a lot about comics.

"General advice to writers: Don't limit yourself to one avenue. Comics aren't really a writer's medium anyway. Write prose, poetry, articles, reviews, screenplays, *anything*. Stay loose. Push yourself. And you may discover some other kind of writing that will support you and fulfill you even if you don't get into comics.

"The *most* general advice: *Just write.* Write comic-book scripts that you think may never be published. Write novels that no-one but you could ever find interesting. Write journals. Write histories of the fall of the Capetian Dynasty in France, even if you don't *know* anything about the fall of the Capetian Dynasty in France. But write things that you care about, or can have fun with, not what you think other people want, because without the fire of enthusiasm, anything that you write - no matter how cleverly imitative of what's selling - is going to be *boring*. Find your passion and then just write and write, and show your writing to people, lots of people, and read it out loud at parties, and take the criticism - positive or negative - as part of the education. Somehow, someday, things *will* happen."

Previous page: A panel from The Trouble with Girls, *penciled by Tim Hamilton, inked by Jim Houghton, and written by creators Will Jacobs and Gerard Jones.*

Gary Kato

Gary Kato collaborated with writer Ron Fortier on Ocean Comics' Mr. Jigsaw *and* The Original Street Fighter *and was an art assistant to Terry Beatty on the much-missed* Ms. Tree. *Gary also contributed pencils, inks, colors to Warp Graphics'* Elfquest: Bedtime Stories *collection, and lettering to the* Elfquest *series* Shards *and* Blood of Ten Chiefs.

Date and place of birth:
December 9th, 1949; Honolulu, Hawaii.

First exposure to comics:
"My first exposure to comics was in the comic-strip section of the Sunday newspaper. The first comic *books* that I remember reading were ones that I got from relatives or family friends. I can recall an issue of *Tom and Jerry* and issues of *Hopalong Cassidy* and *Batman*."

Breaking in:
"While growing up, my brothers and I created homemade comic books for the entertainment of both ourselves and our friends. Later, I began contributing to fanzines, while also submitting an occasional portfolio to the professional publishers. Although most of the fanzine jobs were freebies, the work was valuable to me in that it helped me hone my skills by keeping me drawing all those years. Equally importantly, the contacts and friendships that I established over the years proved invaluable in getting me job offers and recommendations.

"For example, I met writer Ron Fortier when I illustrated one of his short stories for a fanzine. Since then we've collaborated on numerous projects. My association with Terry Beatty began after he saw my work in a fanzine and subsequently asked me to be a part of one of his projects.

"Even the agency that I work through, Star*Reach Productions, has a long-running connection. Its president, Mike Friedrich, was originally a publisher. I made several submissions to his magazine. Although nothing of mine was ever published there, Mike and I did stay in contact - and here we are today.

"The bottom line is that perseverance pays off, not just in terms of learning the craft, but also in establishing a network of friends and acquaintances in the comic-book industry."

Advice to aspiring creators:

To the artist:

• "Keep drawing. Learn to draw anything and everything. You'll never know what a story will require you to depict. And since most comic-book stories are about people, put special emphasis on learning to draw the human figure - *all* aspects of it: Physical appearance, movement and gesture, and thoughts and emotions.

• "Apply your drawing skills to actual stories, so that you can master the craft of breaking your plot into concise page segments composed of smoothly flowing panel-to-panel transitions.

To all creators:

• "Further your education, not just in comic-book-related skills, but in other fields as well. Broadening your education will increase your employment options. After all, you'll need a 'day job' to tide you over until you actually break into the business. And, if nothing else, the learning and knowledge you'll acquire will give you an expanded, fuller perspective of the world. Your life will be enriched and made more enjoyable, and your art and writing will be the better for it.

• "Show your creations, either through the mail or at face-to-face meetings, to editors, publishers, artists, and writers in the comic-book business. This is the only way that you'll get feedback on how your efforts measure up to professional standards."

Above: A panel from Elfquest: Bedtime Stories, *drawn by Gary Kato and written by Terry Beatty and Wendi Lee.*

Barbara Randall Kesel

Barbara Randall Kesel has been a staff editor at both DC and Dark Horse, oversee-
ing such titles as Watchmen, Booster Gold, 'Mazing Man, *and* The New Teen
Titans *at the former and* Instant Piano, Hellboy, *and* Star Wars: Dark Empire
at the latter. Her writing credits include DC's Batgirl *and* Hawk and Dove, *as*
well as Comics' Greatest World: Golden City *and* Will to Power *for Dark*
Horse, where she was a member of the CGW development team.

Date and place of birth:
  October 2nd, 1960; Renton, Washington.

First exposure to comics:
  Barbara vividly remembers "a coverless copy of *Aquaman* #7 found in a
used book store in Seabrook, Texas," as the first comic book that she bought
and read on her own.

Breaking in:
  "I'm probably the only person in the comics business because of a stalker.
  "At nineteen, I was wandering down an open-air antique mall in
Pomona, California, when this guy started walking with me, making some
very strange and sinister suggestions that I listened to calmly while watching for an opportunity for a clean escape.
  "The first open store that I spotted was Pfeiffer's Books and 'Tiques. I
bolted away, ran through the store, ducked in-between the stacks, and
yelled out to the startled couple running the store, 'I'm not here! You don't
see me!' My pal followed, asking the couple if they'd seen his 'girlfriend'.
They pointed to the far door and said that I'd gone that way.
  "They asked if I wanted to call the police, but this was in the days before
people were savvy to the ways of sexual harassment; I figured that all
that'd come of any complaint was that this guy might be able to get my
name and number, so I declined. But I bought one of every DC comic on
the stands behind them.
  "I'd always liked comics, but that was the first time in my life that I'd had
a local source for new ones. I went home, read my comics, liked 'em, and
kept coming back for more.
  "One day, after listening to my latest rant about the state of current
comics, [one of the owners] reminded me gently that I could write to the
companies and tell them. Boinnnng! *Duh!* So I went home and wrote a

ten-page letter telling [DC's then-executive editor] Dick Giordano how to do comics. I was a drama major at Cal Poly Pomona at the time, and God's gift to directing and character analysis…

"Dick *called* me and asked how far I was from San Diego, and if I could go meet him when he was down there at the [annual San Diego] convention. Well, we met and we talked, and after turning down a job - I wanted to finish my degree - I went home with an assignment to write Batgirl backups. Then I graduated, and, while trying to figure out what to do with my life, figured that saying 'Yes' the next time Dick offered a job wouldn't be a bad place to start."

Barbara was offered the job, and accepted it. During and after her time at DC, she says, "I fell in love, got married, went freelance, went crazy working in a basement office [while freelancing], took another day job at Dark Horse, watched the company grow from fifteen to a hundred-odd, got stressed, decided to 'retire' way early, and am back to writing and wandering the world lost in thought."

Advice to aspiring creators:

"Artists: Try to gain some point of view outside of comics. The most interesting and influential artists in comics are those who never stop testing their own limits, and who never used - or have broken away from - the crutch of swiping. Be prepared to do lots of samples, be ready to hear lots of contradictory advice, but stick with it. There is no *one way* to do comics, so you have to listen to your own inner muse for direction - yet remain aware that most comics are produced with a commercial end in mind, so current market considerations will dictate what kind of art is chosen and nurtured. If you have a strong vision, stick with it. If you're in it to make a living from whoever's paying, be flexible.

"Writers: It's harder, since an editor can't look at a page of script the way one can look at a page of art and know if i''s going to work or not. The biggest mistake that I see new writers make is that they develop an attitude before they develop their skills. Be ready to have your work butchered by amateur artists - you're both learning. Enjoy your successes, but analyze your failures. If the artist failed to bring your story to life, could something in your script have made your intent unclear? Rather than spend your time on blind submissions to big companies, start small. Find a small publisher willing to work with you, or find a new artist who will. You'll find it much easier to break in with complete packages, story and art, rather than just a story."

Previous page: A scene from Mike Mignola's Hellboy.

Jeffrey Lang

Jeffrey Lang has written for Caliber Press' Creatures of the Id, *Now Comics'* Twilight Zone, *and Warner International Publishing's* Looney Tunes *and* Tiny Toon Adventures. *He is the writer and co-creator of* Roadways, *first released as a mini-series by Cult Press, and of the* Nanny Katie *stories, which have appeared in* Negative Burn *and* Dark Horse Presents. *Jeff's current projects include* Underside *and a story arc in* The Jam, *both coming from Caliber next year.*

Date and place of birth:
August 18th, 1960; Reading, Pennsylvania.

First exposure to comics:
"The first comic that I remember clearly was an issue of *Daredevil* that my brother Mike had bought from some kid in school. It was a story about how the Jester convinced everyone that Daredevil had murdered him. It had Gene Colan art, I was six years old, and it was like nothing I had ever seen. Probably my mother or grandmother had bought us Bugs Bunny or Donald Duck comics before then, but I had pretty much ignored them. I remember thinking how weird it was that [Daredevil] was blind, but was still able to get around.

"That comic began a nearly twenty-year cycle where I had to read almost everything with the Marvel logo. I got over it about ten years ago. I eventually branched out into some DC stuff, then the indies of the '80s."

Breaking in:
"In my senior year in college - which eventually stretched into three years - I got a job working at the comics shop that I'd been haunting for the past couple of years, a place called the Book Swap in State College, Pennsylvania. (It's now called the Comic Swap and is owned by a kid I sold comics to. Hi, Kris!)

"After doing that for five years, during which I had graduated and gotten married, I decided that it was time to try to figure out what I really wanted to do with my life, so I wrote a letter to Diana Schutz at Comico - which was then located in the outskirts of Philadelphia - and got a job as Bob Schreck's assistant. That situation lasted about a year.

"Working at Comico taught me a lot of important things, but probably one of the most important was that writing wasn't as hard as it had once seemed. Just before I started working for Comico, I sent some sample reviews to Kevin Dooley, then the editor of *Amazing Heroes*, and though he didn't publish them, he did send back some nice comments about them. I decided to submit some more reviews, and - surprise, surprise - they accepted them. Shortly after that, I sold Caliber on the idea of a collection of three short stories by Michael Allred, Bernie Mireault, and me.

"Somewhere along the line, I met Patricia Jeres, and when she got set up at DC, she asked me to write articles that she [as manager of marketing communications] then placed in a variety of trade magazines. That's consumed a lot of time over the past few years, time that might have been devoted to more creative endeavors, but it's given me the opportunity to talk to some of the most interesting people in this business, so it was worth it."

Advice to aspiring creators:

"Before you can learn to write, you have to learn to read. Writers have to be readers. Learn something about story structure before starting to write, which essentially means 'Do a lot of reading.' All of the Joseph Campbell essays in the world won't mean a thing until you have some context.

"Be prepared for the fact that comics is one of the most difficult fields in which to be a writer - or perhaps I should say '*just* a writer'. Bernie Mireault once told me that he learned to draw because he wanted to write comics. He might really have something there.

"Whatever your goal, persevere - and don't let the comments of some mallet-brained editor discourage you. Take good critical advice when you can get it, but don't let the rejections discourage you, especially if you're trying to do something beyond the norm. A good piece of writing is a transcendental experience - which is the only reason anyone would ever put in all the time and effort that it can cost."

Right: The title character of Jeffrey Lang and Steven Leiber's Nanny Katie *stories.*

Batton Lash

Batton Lash is best known for Wolff and Byrd, Counselors of the Macabre, *which began life as a comic strip over fifteen years ago and was recently launched in comic-book form by Batton's own Exhibit 'A' Press. Bat also wrote the Archie Comics/Marvel Comics crossover* Archie Meets the Punisher, *and has illustrated entries in the* Big Book of… *series (Death, Weirdos, Urban Legends) for Paradox Press.*

Date and place of birth:
October 29th, 1953; Brooklyn, New York.

First exposure to comics:
"I seem to recall Superman-family titles and Batman in *Detective Comics* among the first comics I ever saw. I also remember being taken with *Dick Tracy*, early on, in 1959 or so. I was doing my own little comics using my dad's scratch pads and staplers soon after that."

Breaking in:
"'Breaking in' is the right expression! I feel like I snuck in the basement window of the industry when no-one was looking…

"A local newspaper, *The Brooklyn Paper*, asked me to do a weekly strip for them in 1979. It was *Wolff and Byrd*, and I've been doing it ever since - still fine-tuning the thing, too!

"When the first [*Wolff and Byrd*] collection came out in 1987, I began going to conventions to promote it. Shoving my mug around often enough, I made contacts [and] got some work to subsidize *Wolff and Byrd*, so I guess I really 'broke in' over a fifteen-year span."

Advice to aspiring creators:
"Don't let anyone discourage you!
Comics is a tough business and there are quite a
few characters in the industry who enjoy chewing up the 'new' kid and

spitting him out. Don't let it get to you. Just do what your gut instinct tells you. Follow your own impulses. If you try to second-guess the 'market', the end result will look like… well, like you're second-guessing!

"If you *really* want to do comics, like *I* did, there are plenty of avenues available: The local [community or small-press] newspaper is one. The pay won't be great, but you'll get to see what your work looks like reproduced. It's like your out-of-town performances before you take your show to Broadway.

"Create your own series - something that only *you* can do. Carve your own niche, rather than follow someone else's lead. And *own* it, too!"

Above: Batton Lash's offbeat creations Wolff and Byrd. Previous page: The icon designed for Archie Meets the Punisher.

Stan Lee

Stan Lee created, along with such legendary artists as Jack Kirby and Steve Ditko, the foundations of what is today known as the Marvel Universe. He began his career over fifty-five years ago at Marvel Comics' predecessor, Timely, where his first work appeared in Captain America. *He went on to write and edit such series as* Strange Tales, Journey into Mystery, *and* Tales to Astonish, *and in the early 1960s launched* The Fantastic Four, The Amazing Spider-Man, The Incredible Hulk, Daredevil, Iron Man, The Avengers, The X-Men, Sgt. Fury, *and many, many more. He is currently the publisher and spiritual leader of Marvel Comics - which is preparing to launch a new line of Lee-created comic books, titled Excelsior - and continues to write the Spider-Man newspaper strip.*

Date and place of birth:
December 28th, 1922; New York, New York.

Breaking in:
"I answered an ad. Things were different in '39, the year that I broke in. Publishers actually occasionally *advertised* for writers and editors."

Advice to aspiring creators:
"Keep studying! Keep practicing! Keep submitting!"

Above: Spider-Man, one of Stan Lee's many Marvelous characters, as rendered by John Byrne.

Tom Lyle

Tom Lyle has drawn Sky Wolf *and* Strike *for Eclipse,* Robin *and* Starman *for DC, and* Spider-Man *and* The Punisher *for Marvel. He makes his debut as a solo writer with the upcoming* Spider-Man/Punisher *crossover.*

Date and Place of Birth:
November 2nd, 1953; Jacksonville, Florida.

First exposure to comics:
"I was a big Ditko fan, and *Spider-Man* was one of the first Marvel comics that I read," Tom recalls. And it was chance encounter: Marvels were poorly distributed in Jacksonville, Tom says. "I just managed by chance one day to encounter a *Spider-Man*, and I thought, 'Cool, I have to find *more* of this stuff!'"

Breaking in:
"I had sort-of made half-hearted attempts throughout my entire career [in ad design]; I would send in my portfolio, get rejected, and crawl into a hole for about a year, and then send off another portfolio. When I was thirty, I had to figure out if I was really willing to make a go of it, and my wife was willing to help. We moved to Baltimore with no jobs so that I could be closer to New York City and go in and show my work more often. It's tough to do that over the phone and through the mail."

Sure enough, Tom landed his first pro comics job through personal contact. "I ran into Chuck Dixon at a Serendipity show in Philadelphia; I knew him from his *Evangeline* stuff, and *Airboy* had just started coming out. I was working for David Campiti at the time, doing stuff on Wonder Color Comics - *GI Rambot* and *Power Factor*, two great comics! Chuck talked to Tim Truman, who was the editor on *Airboy* at the time, and he wanted me to work for them. The biggest obstacle to my working for them was [Eclipse editor-in-chief] Cat Yronwode, because Cat's response to Chuck and Tim was that I was 'too Marvel'. But they didn't think that it would *hurt* to have a Marvel style on the books..."

Advice to aspiring creators:
"It's especially difficult now that the market has crashed so badly. There are so few books now; just about a year ago, they were hiring anybody who could hold a pencil, and now people I *know* are out of work.

"You have to be persistent, and that means showing your stuff as often as possible at conventions. I think that conventions are the best places to show your work now. You would not *believe* how many mail submissions the publishers get these days; it's such a huge pile that you'll just never get looked at. I know that they try - they genuinely do try to look at everybody's stuff - but it's darn near impossible to cover as many people as they'd like. So I'd say to try conventions where editorial people are going to be. The only reason that you need to bother showing [work] to other artists is to get their opinions of where you stand in the industry; they can't offer you any assignments, just criticisms and comments and advice. The *editors* have the jobs.

"A lot of people who show their samples show too many pages; I would narrow it down to five to six pages at most. I wouldn't bother showing any pin-up stuff at all; they *all* need to be story pages. Also, if you're carrying the same samples around for a month, you're making a mistake - every time you show your work to an editor, you should have different samples, which means that you have to get down to the drawing board and draw some, whether you like it or not. That was the hardest part for me, drawing new samples all the time," Tom remembers with a laugh. "'Man, I'm not even getting *paid* for this…!' But don't be discouraged by how much time it might take. Those samples may seem slower than Christmas, but it's amazing how *fast* it goes once you're getting paid and you have a deadline to meet."

Above: Another view of Spider-Man, with the Punisher and drawn by Tom Lyle.

Stan Lynde

Stan Lynde is a cartoonist's cartoonist, one of the most revered creators in the business and the recipient of an Inkpot Award for Achievement in the Comic Arts. Stan's syndicated comic strips Rick O'Shay *and* Latigo *ran for a combined total of twenty-five years, and are available in collected form - as is his acclaimed book of memoirs,* Rick O'Shay, Hipshot, and Me *- from Cottonwood Graphics, published by Stan with his wife, Lynda Brown Lynde.*

Date and place of birth:
September 23rd, 1931; Billings, Montana.

First exposure to comics:
"My parents read the newspaper strips, and especially the Sunday comics, to me," Stan says. "When I discovered - at about age five or six - that *people* actually produced that wonderful stuff, it was like a religious revelation. *I* wanted to do that!

"I idolized Hal Foster's work on *Prince Valiant*, and Al Capp's *Li'l Abner* - and I was totally blown away by the adventures of Batman and Superman. I first saw them in *Detective* and *Action Comics*, then in their own books, both of which I owned and traded away. Who knew?"

Breaking in:
Stan created comics throughout grade school to entertain himself and friends, and later translated that experience into a job producing the comic strip *Ty Phoon* for his Navy newspaper, *The Marianas Mariner*. He attended the New York School of Visual Arts, and studied under Burne Hogarth, Jerry Robinson, and other comics professionals, finally landing his own nationally syndicated strip, *Rick O'Shay*, with the *Chicago Tribune-New York News* Syndicate in 1958. He broke into the comic-book market itself publishing reprints of his strips.

Advice to aspiring creators:
"Do what *you* love *your* way. Get the best training that you can, *however* you can. Practice, practice, practice; believe in yourself, and *persist*. That about sums it up!"

John MacLeod

John MacLeod has published ten issues of The Mundane Adventures of Dishman *to date, all written and drawn by himself. A collection of the first six issues was published by Eclipse Comics, and he's now at work on a variety of projects - including more* Dishman.

Date and place of birth:
   April 24th, 1957; Brantford, Ontario.

First exposure to comics:
   "I started reading newspaper funnies in 1960 at age three, supplemented by comic books from my parents. I remember *Dennis the Menace, Little Lulu, Mighty Mouse,* various Disney and Harvey titles - and I'm *sure* that there was a *Peanuts* comic book back then, I remember it so vividly.
   "When I was seven, I was introduced to 'serious comics' by a school chum with a pile of DCs, and from that point on I was hooked. The following year, I met another guy with Marvels and that just made it worse! Ever since, it's never been a question of *if* I read comics, just *how many* and *which ones...*"

Breaking in:
   "In 1983 or '84, somewhere in there, *The Comics Journal* ran a series of articles on the small press and small-press creators. This was the first that I had ever heard of such a thing, and I was amazed by the whole concept of self-publishing on a modest scale. I wrote to quite a few of the creators mentioned therein. Of all of them, Chester Brown was the one who gave above and beyond the call of duty; he corresponded with me voluminously for months, answering a multitude of dumb niggly questions, and connecting me with contacts in the small-press network. Thanks in large part to Chester, by August 1985 I had published my first small-press 'zine. If you count

small press as ' breaking in' - which I do - then that's how I broke in, like any *other* small-presser: I just *did it*.

"By 1986, during the black-and-white indy boom, the small-press *Dishman* was being carried by five distributors in North America and Europe, so a lot of people were seeing it, and a number of indy publishers were inquiring about reprint rights. Scott McCloud, who is on my mailing list and who has supported me a *lot*, suggested that I send *Dishman* to the people at Eclipse Comics, [then] his publisher, just because he thought that they might enjoy it. So I did - and Eclipse ended up *also* asking about reprint rights. As it turned out, Eclipse offered me the best deal, so it ended up publishing the *Dishman* reprint collection. And that's how I broke into 'big press', again thanks to another creator pushing me."

Advice to aspiring creators:
"I can think of no better advice than this: Read *Understanding Comics* by Scott McCloud over and over again until you absorb it, internalize it - until it becomes a part of you. Armed with the principles of that book, you will have the awareness to strive for mastery of the art of comics, and the freedom to find your own personal contribution to the field. There is no more important piece of work in the entire medium of comics than that book.

"But of course I can't leave it at that…

• "When learning to draw comics, look at more than just other comics - *and* more than genre fiction and genre film and TV.

• "Study old masters of comics, like Roy Crane and Alex Toth. Learn your history.

• "Study Japanese comics, especially those that don't look a lot like American ones.

• "If small press interests you, *do it now*. There's no need to wait. If you're 'not there yet', there's plenty of folks in the network who'll provide constructive criticism to help you along. The experience of actually doing it, making it, getting it out there, and getting feedback is invaluable, fulfilling, and great fun.

• "If you aspire primarily to 'big press', then I have no advice. *I'm* certainly no example to follow; all of my forays into big press have literally fallen into my lap, and I've never had the time or energy to make the big push into increasing my momentum and getting into it full-time. Actually, maybe *that's* my advice: Big-press work demands *a lot* of time and energy, so make sure that you have them *and* make sure that you really want to give them."

David Mazzucchelli

David Mazzucchelli stunned readers with his work on Marvel's Daredevil: Fall from Grace *and DC's* Batman: Year One, *both written by Frank Miller, before moving on to publishing his and others' more avant-garde work in the anthology series* Rubber Blanket. *He has written and illustrated stories for Drawn and Quarterly's eponymous anthology and Fantagraphics'* Zero Zero, *and recently adapted Paul Auster's* City of Glass *to comics form for Avon's Neon Lit imprint.*

First Exposure to Comics:
   David has drawings of his dating back to the age of five, when he would copy the newspaper comics in ball-point pen. What caught his eye? "*Peanuts, Buz Sawyer, Henry, Nancy,* John Romita's Spider-Man fighting the Kingpin - the first time," he says. Rounding out his early comics memories: "*Marvel Superheroes* and *Batman* on TV *and* in comic books; a Batman comic drawn in crayon at age six; *Peanuts* collections in paperback; *Gnatman* [a *Batman* parody] in *Not Brand Ecch*... It all grew from there."

Breaking In:
   "While in college, studying painting, I would periodically send sample pages to Marvel and DC, and receive encouraging rejections. Eventually I visited a convention in New York, where I got some very good critiques and advice from professionals. By the time I graduated, Jim Shooter, then editor-in-chief at Marvel, had given me a fill-in job to pencil. After convincing [Marvel] that I could do better than that first job, I started getting steady work - first a series of one-shot stories, and then the regular assignment on *Daredevil*."

Advice to Aspiring Creators:
   "Don't limit the sources of your inspiration to comics alone. Of course you should be well-versed in comics - that's the discipline you've chosen to work in - but your own work and the field as a whole benefits from knowledge of things outside comics: Art, design, literature, music, summer job experiences, recipes, *anything*. A personal voice will last longer than a trendy style.
   "And don't get cocky. All of us still have things to learn."

Terry Moore

Terry Moore is the creator, writer, artist, and now publisher - through his own Abstract Studio - of Strangers in Paradise, *which began life as a mini-series at Antarctic Press. He has also contributed to Caliber Press'* Negative Burn, *Fantagraphics Books'* Real Stuff, *and DC Comics/Vertigo's* The Endless Gallery.

Date and place of birth:
November 19th, 1954; Texas.

First exposure to comics:
Terry's earliest comic-book memories involve Superman and Batman, but, he says, "My first real comic addiction was Spider-Man, in the '60s."

Breaking in:
After some false starts trying to create and market his own comic strip, Terry decided to forego the newspaper route and flesh out his concepts in comic *books*. "I showed the first issue of *Strangers in Paradise*, to everybody I could," he says. "I went to cons, I met people… I had a very good response from artists and editors alike, so I knew to keep trying.

"I was about to self-publish when I got a call from Antarctic Press. [Antarctic] offered to print a three-part mini-series, so we did. That got got me a book in my hands, and I was set up with the distributors. When I finally did self-publish, my book was already basically established."

Advice to aspiring creators:
• "If you want to work for another publisher, you need to be professional in your approach and your business manners from the beginning. Know who you're talking to: Don't show hero work to Karen Berger

INTERESTING.

[executive editor of Vertigo] and don't show stories about relationships to [Image Comics publisher] Tony Lobito.

• "Don't bother showing pin-up work to editors. They want artists and writers who can *tell stories*.

• "If you want to self-publish you must know and understand retailers and distributors. They are your business partners and first-line customers.

• "Be original. Notice how the really popular books right now - *Spawn*, *Gen 13*, *Sin City*, and *Bone* - are all completely different from one another. I see *so many* young creators trying to break in with material that I've seen done already. Everybody should be looking for something new and original.

• "If you're trying to break in with a book about a renegade group of mutant misfits who join together to battle for a dark type of justice in a cruel world, then *nobody* can help you. Wake up and smell the burnout."

Above and previous page: Artwork from Terry Moore's Strangers in Paradise.

Doug Murray

Doug Murray is the acclaimed writer/creator of Marvel Comics' The 'Nam. *He has also written Marvel's* Conan *and* Nick Fury, Agent of SHIELD, *Disney's* Roger Rabbit *and* Darkwing Duck, *and the DC graphic novel* Batman: Digital Justice.

Date and place of birth:
November 13th, 1947; Brooklyn, New York.

First exposure to comics:
"I grew up when comics were only available in the corner drugstore. My first comic book was *Mystery in Space* #1, because it had an adaptation of *Destination Moon*. Later, I became a reader of most of the DC titles."

Breaking in:
"I spent some time working around the Neal Adams studios in the '70s, doing this and that, and got friendly with all the guys there. One of them was Larry Hama, and when he became an editor at Marvel and needed a Vietnam vet who knew comics... I started by doing stories for *Savage Tales*, used that as a springboard for *The 'Nam*, and have been working steadily since."

Advice to aspiring creators:
"It's tough to break into comics, especially for writers - an editor has to actually spend some time *reading* your stuff to find out if you have any talent. You've got to be willing to take rejection to break in, and even then you may have to self-publish or work through a small company. Anything that works. If you can't put up with that, you're never going to make it."

Left: Doug Murray's crimefighting alter-ego.

Jeff Nicholson

Jeff Nicholson is the creator, writer, artist, and publisher of Ultra Klutz, Lost Laughter, *and the softcover collections* Through the Habitrails *and* Nicholson's Small-Press Tirade. *His current project is the ongoing series* Father and Son, *published by Kitchen Sink Press.*

Date and place of birth:
October 5th, 1962; Walnut Creek, California.

First exposure to comics:
"When I was in second grade or so, one of my older cousins had a magazine rack full of *Mad* magazines," Jeff remembers. "Several years later I became a Superman fan and collected DC comics by the thousands, but that type of material never influenced my work like the old *Mad*s did."

Breaking in:
"I self-published an underground at age eighteen, which was a complete failure. Two years later, I started submitting very primitive work to the newly forming independents. My first acceptance came from Comico, but it canceled its anthology title, *Primer*, before my work saw print. I then turned to self-publishing photocopied small-press comics with *Ultra Klutz and Other Tales* in 1984. I published five issues and gained a lot of valuable experience and feedback.

"With [*Cerebus* cerator/self-publisher] Dave Sim as my role model, I decided that it was time to launch the series as an independent title. By sheer luck, this was the spring of 1986, the peak of the black-and-white speculation frenzy. *Ultra Klutz* #1 sold very well. The demand for independents later crashed, but my foot in the market was established."

Advice to aspiring creators:
"These suggestions are for the would-be writer/artist of alternative or independent material:

"Don't just make proposals. Make comics. Labor yourself over finished, reproducible pages, even if you don't have a particular publisher or outlet in mind. I have a sketchbook that I used from 1984 to 1994, and it is only half-full. In that same time period, I produced well over one-thousand published pages of comic art. Other artists may have chosen to fill five sketchbooks and produce four-hundred pages in that same timeframe.

Sketchbooks are fine for occasionally brushing up on drapery, faces, etc., but don't live in them. Do the real thing.

"Know that you are committing yourself to a life of possible poverty with no 'benefits' or 'retirement plan'. Day jobs, if needed, must be mindless labor with low stress, so as not to drain your precious drive to create comics. Realizing this, it is important not to let any external forces, such as editors or publishers, alter your work beyond your personal vision, since there isn't enough money at stake to do so.

"Take pride, soldier."

Above: A panel from Jeff Nicholson's Ultra Klutz.

Turtel Onli

Turtel Onli has provided illustrations for Paris Metro, Oui, *and* Mode Avant-Garde *and album-cover art for George Clinton and Curtis Blow. Through Onli Studios, he has published the comic books* Nog, Protector of the Pyramids *and* Sustah-Girl, Queen of the Black Age, *among others.*

Date and place of birth:
January 25th, 1952; Chicago, Illinois.

First exposure to comics:
"In the late '50s I read copies of *The Human Torch and Toro* and the Jack Kirby monster titles. My family members were artistic, but none were pros, so I decided to be the first pro in my family. I felt that I could be a 'black Jack Kirby' if I could get the support."

Breaking in:
"For most of my career, I found 'whites' too uneasy to hire me and 'blacks' too provincial to accept my innovations. It is hard to grow when you make people uptight by being yourself. But the work of Kirby and his rough life inspired me."

Turtel earned an MAAT in art therapy from the Art Institute of Chicago and began a career as an illustrator, doing editorial work and courtroom sketches for a local television station. His first professional art job was for *PTA Magazine.*

"I started self-publishing in the '70s and crated 'the Black Age of Comics' in the '80s," he says. "But I'm still very much an outsider looking in."

Advice to aspiring creators:
"Study everything and everybody that touches you, past, present, or future. There's no one path to success. And have a life *outside* of comics and creativity.

"Hire yourself - that's the American dream. Free enterprise lives."

Jerry Ordway

Jerry Ordway was for years one of the guiding forces behind DC Comics' Super-man titles. He has written, penciled, and/or inked The Fantastic Four *for Marvel,* WildStar *for Image, and* All-Star Squadron, Infinity Inc., Superman, *and* The Adventures of Superman *for DC. He is currently writing DC's* The Power of Shazam, *an ongoing series that follows Jerry's acclaimed painted graphic novel of the same title.*

Date and place of birth:
November 28th, 1957, "Thanksgiving Eve, in a speeding car, headed for the hospital"; Milwaukee, Wisconsin.

First exposure to comics:
"I watched the *Marvel Superheroes* cartoons on TV in the late '60s; they were choppy, but I thought that they were pretty good, and I started drawing from them. I then wound up, while going to my brother's college graduation in 1967, finding Marvel comics on the newsstands - and I was totally stunned that they made comics of the cartoons that I liked! I was a hardcore Marvel fan throughout the '70s."

Breaking in:
"I made a trip to New York City in 1977 with Mike Machlan and a couple of other people, looking for work. I hadn't quite turned twenty yet. We got there about two weeks before DC had the implosion, when a lot of the books were canceled and they fired a lot of people, so we didn't get work then. I was annoyed; during the trip, the only high point was that Jim Shooter, at Marvel, had given us a bunch of Xeroxes of pencils to practice inking with, which was really a lot of fun. But I decided to forget comics and try to get into commercial art.

"I stopped doing comics samples, and started painting. I got work at an art studio where I worked my way up from the stat department; I'd never gone to art school, so this was my schooling. ... The studio worked with Western Publishing, and, ironically, I ended up working on a DC-superhe-roes activity book, so I had to do samples for DC Comics. DC approved them, and Western was totally thrilled because they could have *new* art instead of using clip art. On top of that, Western had Marvel books to do, so I got the chance to do a four-part Marvel series that had to with reading, writing, and arithmetic.

"The samples from the DC book I took to a Chicago Comicon in 1980. I was showing them to Joe Orlando, who was totally burnt out and couldn't figure out why the stars on Wonder Woman's costume were missing - that was one of the games, the stars were hidden - when Paul Levitz came up telling Joe that he'd been at it too long and *had* to break for dinner; Paul looked down at my samples, saw my name, and said, 'Oh, Jerry Ordway. We've been trying to get in touch with you.' I came within inches of being turned down by Joe Orlando, and Paul Levitz came along saying that he had work for me!

"About a week later, DC sent me a six-page story to ink over Carmine Infantino that was for the revamped *Mystery in Space*; I inked that after work, because I was still working a full-time job at this art studio. I eventually left that job when DC offered me *All-Star Squadron* [inking] Rich Buckler, whose work I liked - I'd been a big fan of his. And I kept bugging DC to let me pencil something until they did."

Advice to aspiring creators:
"Don't let anybody shake your confidence if you like what you're doing. A lot of people who give you advice are trying to shake you from your dream. When they do that, there's a realistic point to it - not everybody's going to get into comics; very few people walk in and hear, 'Hey, this guy's great; put him on *Spider-Man*.' But if you have the fortitude, if you stick with it, maybe something will happen.

"Rob Liefeld skyrocketed very fast, but Rob was actually around a long time. I knew Rob when he was doing his fan stuff, working with the Teen Titans fan club. For him, it was a meteoric rise, once he got that first job. But a lot of people will get that first job, get their foot in the door, and not make any further inroads for years. Getting that first job may be

followed by ten years of struggling just to land your first series.

"A lot of editors are looking at samples at convention tables and are saying, 'Don't ever do this; don't ever do that.' And, quite honestly, there are a lot of editors who don" draw, and *they* shouldn't be giving you art advice. Maybe they'll say, 'Your pencils are good, why are you bothering to ink?' That's a lot of BS. Whether it's pencils, inks, or colors, it's your decision and your growth. Sure, you should concentrate on what might land you a job, but you don't want to limit yourself.

"If someone says to you, 'Your perspective is off,' maybe you should work on your perspective. But if someone says, 'I don't like the way you draw,' maybe you should get another opinion."

Above: A painted shot of Captain Marvel from Jerry Ordway's The Power of Shazam. *Previous page: Jerry's rendition of two of the world's mightiest mortals.*

Shea Anton Pensa

Shea Anton Pensa broke into the American comics industry from his native Australia with work on Green Arrow, The Butcher, *and the revival of* The Brave and the Bold *for DC Comics. His more recent work includes* The Punisher *for Marvel and a sequence in the DC/Vertigo collection* The Sandman: World's End. *He's currently at work painting a "James Cameron-style" science-fiction epic of his own creation.*

Date and place of birth:
   March 18th, 1968; Sydney, New South Wales.

Breaking in:
   "I decided that I was going to do comic books when I was eight-and-a-half years old. And that was it - I started learning all that I could: Looking at the work of Kirby and Ditko, finding out what all of the terms meant. ... By the time I was nine-and-a-half, I understood the difference between inker, colorist, editor, writer, penciler, and whatnot. By ten, I was refining my inking technique, because I knew that a bad inker could ruin good pencils, and there were a lot of inkers whom, even at ten, I didn't like. I was afraid that the editor would give me a bad inker, so I wanted to make my inks as professional as possible as early as possible instead of risking a bad inker.
   "I started panel-by-panel drawings by the time I was thirteen-and-a-half, and I started preparing real comic-book layout, finding out the appropriate sizes and papers, by the time I was sixteen. I completed a forty-eight-page piece, penciled, inked, and written by myself, which was definitely not publishable - but at least I'd put in the effort, and I traveled up to Eclipse to see if they'd hire me. [That was at] seventeen years old. I'd submitted pencils to Marvel when I was sixteen, then moved back to my native country of Australia when I was eighteen, and my work was good enough to get me published there, in 1986, in *Cyclone Comics*.
   "Mike Baron was hanging out with the *Cyclone* boys, putting together a promotion for *Badger*. He'd seen my work and liked it, and wrote a letter to the *Cyclone* boys complementing it. I really appreciated the letter, so I got his address and wrote him a thank-you, and he then told me that if I was ever in America he and I should hook up and he was very interested in working with me, because my approach to comics was, he felt, very different. I took that as a cue, packed up all of my [stuff], and moved to

America. I gave Mike a call within the first month. I was nineteen then, turned twenty soon afterwards, and Mike set me up with my first American gig, which was a six-page backup in *Nexus* #51 featuring Judah Macabee.

"I got it in my head that eventually I would have to paint when I caught on to some old *Heavy Metals* and some old Marvel/Epics that were well-painted, and I saw the difference in atmosphere and mood. And for the stories that I knew that I wanted to write myself, I knew that I would need the painted medium. For the longest time I never believed that I could [paint], and I was eighteen before I started seriously dabbling in watercolor. By the time I was twenty-two, I had moved on to acrylics, oils, mixed media, stuff like that; it went pretty quickly."

Advice to aspiring creators:

"Comics now is totally cutthroat; it's a little entertainment industry, a little Hollywood. The age for being successful and 'making it' has dropped every year. Most of the guys who are making it now were already in by the time they were eighteen, like I was.

"If [aspiring creators] have their sights set on things like the X-Men books or something for Image or a high-profile artsy book for Dark Horse then I think that, unfortunately, it's mandatory for them to sink their teeth into it like a pit bull and start as *soon* as they make that decision - find out types of paper, take life-drawing classes, study Eisner, find resources. By the time they're sixteen - and this might sound a *little* extreme - it's time to start going to cons and making the appropriate friends. ...

"I think that self-publishing is a strong option in terms of keeping true to a vision and even making a profit *if your work is marketable*. However, people do see a stigma with self-publishing - although it's going away, thank God - of it being a last resort for people who can't get published elsewhere. I don't think that it's a wise idea for people to self-publish before they have a major credit with someone else and have proved that they can play the game and get the fans; I think that self-publishing is an *excellent* choice for people who have *already* built a fan base with their art or their writing.

"In regards to a creator-owned property at another company, I think that it's good *if* the deal is there and *if* the people are reliable and will publish the book - not fold all of a sudden because they're greedy and they don't like the way that the comics-industry economy is going at a certain point. We've seen *that* happen, and unfortunately if people want to publish under their own company after mainstream success elsewhere, then what happened with Axis Comics or Ominous Press [both of which folded after brief, erratic publication in the months prior to this interview] is no help.

"If you do want to do a creator-owned book or a self-published book where you have total control, then you *need* a good internal editor; you need to be able to look at your work and say, 'It's not good enough.' And you don't get that easily, not without having worked for *real* editors and very, very picky, specific writers. There's always something to learn from working with other people, no matter how strong your creative vision is. What I'm painting right now, for a creator-owned project that I hope to have published soon, would not be anywhere near as good as it is if I hadn't put my time in at DC. Working with Mike Baron, Mike Grell, and Neil Gaiman certainly helped *my* internal editor."

Some more specific advice for artists from Shea:

- "As much as you hate to hear it, you *must* do life-drawing. And you may *think* that you can get away without doing it, you may *think* that your work looks really good, but here's a little secret: When you're showing your portfolio, and you haven't done the life-drawing, *it will show.*

- "Layout - and *good* layout - is coming back. Kids breaking in today don't necessarily need to study the old guys whom I would list - Will Eisner, Wally Wood, Frank Frazetta - but they should at least look at Kirby, some of the good *old* Kirby, from 1965 to 1969. Frank Miller is a good example, too. You should also get used to varying your shots, whether they're up shots, down shots, bird's-eye-view shots, worm's-eye-view shots. Learn establishing shots, because that's a *major* weakness among most of the young artists; it's not fun, so they don't teach themselves to do it, and it shows up in their work.

- "Have a variety in what you can do: Don't just be a sci-fi artist, don't just be a superhero artist, be able to tell a *Jonah Hex* story in addition to being able to tell a *Nexus* story in addition to being able do, like, Marc Silvestri stuff. If you can do three genres, then you triple your chances to get work."

Faye Perozich

Faye Perozich has written Shadowman *and* Magnus: Robot Fighter *for Valiant,* Hellraiser *for Marvel's Epic line,* Bloodchilde *for Millenium, and* Harlan Ellison's Dream Corridor *for Dark Horse. She adapted the Anne Rice novels* Interview with the Vampire, The Vampire Lestat, *and* Queen of the Damned *for Innovation, and* The Mummy *for Millenium.*

Date and place of birth:
   April 27th, 1963; Pittsburgh, Pennsylvania.

First exposure to comics:
   "Although I read my brother's copies of *The Fantastic Four* and *Ghost Rider* when I was young, my love affair with the medium didn't start until much later, when I read *Watchmen*. After that, I was hooked."

Breaking in:
   "I took an office job with Innovation Comics, as office manager and, later, production supervisor. I negotiated for the rights to adapt Anne Rice's *The Vampire Lestat*, and - since I had been writing outside of comics for ten years - was given the assignment to write [the adaptation] myself. It took off, doing well enough to enable me to start freelancing full-time."

Advice to aspiring creators:
   "Too many writers and artists in this business learn to draw or write only by looking at comics, and that gives you a very narrow view of your art. Learn to draw from life; learn to write about real people - *then* take what you have learned and apply it to comics.
   "You might want to learn about different areas of the field, such as production. Many aspiring artists get their feet in the door working in-house first.
   "Above all, don't get discouraged. It can take awhile to get started, and there can be disappointments along the way, but the ride is worth it. If you've got the talent and the drive, you'll make it sooner or later."

Gordon Purcell

Gordon Purcell's credits can be found on DC's Star Trek *and* Star Trek: The Next Generation *, Malibu's* Star Trek: Deep Space Nine*, Dark Horse's* The Young Indiana Jones Chronicles*, and Marvel's* Mad Dog, Wonder Man*, and* The Avengers.

Date and place of birth:
February 14th, 1959; Traverse City, Michigan.

First exposure to comics:
"I loved animated cartoons as a kid, and started picking up Disney and Gold Key comics. I would swap comics with the neighborhood kids, who read DCs and Marvels. My mom threw away all the cartoon comics, but she let me keep one - a Batman comic that my dad bought for me when I was sick."

Breaking in:
"I got my BAs in Studio Arts and Theatre from the University of Minnesota, but the 'normal' job that I had arranged for after college was eliminated. I went to a local comics convention with some samples that I'd put together over a weekend, and got some work doing layouts for Greg Guler on *Sentinels of Justice* for Americomics.

"I did small jobs for small independents, was a finalist in the *Marvel Try-Out Book* contest, joined the DC New Talent Program - all opportunities to learn, although none of these paid off big. Finally, Mike Carlin and Dan Jurgens brought me to Barb Kesel's attention at DC to draw one of the first DC Bonus Books, in *Flash* #12."

Advice to aspiring creators:

"Take art courses, draw from real life, and draw every day. If you want to work in mainstream comics, look at the artists who have strong storytelling abilities - the Buscemas, for example - and not the stylists; you can develop your own style later on. Even Picasso's academic art looked very traditional; once he developed the basic skills, he could go off on his own direction.

"Not everyone breaks in quickly and easily - there is some amount of luck involved. Try to learn from every opportunity. It's good to see your stuff in print, and it's good to learn how to act in a professional manner with your fellow creators.

"Mainstream comic companies want professional creators who can meet deadlines and match mainstream styles. Don't be afraid: There is a much greater variety in art styles in comics nowadays - if you are professional and have some basic skills, you should find work somewhere in comics.

"Good luck!"

Previous Page: A panel from Mad Dog, *penciled by Gordon Purcell and inked by Ian Akin.*

Daniel Reed

Daniel Reed is the writer and illustrator of Retro-Dead, *which he publishes with his wife, Eve Teitelbaum, through Blazer Unlimited. His past professional credits include Blazer's* New World Order *and pencil art on* The Incredible Hulk *and* Alpha Flight *for Marvel.*

Date and place of birth:
January 26th, 1960; Springfield, Massachusetts.

Breaking in:
"When I was about thirteen, I was living in Miami, and I found out that [legendary Captain Marvel artist] CC Beck lived a bus ride away. So I went and sat on his doorstep one day - all day, until his neighbor came out and said, 'He's away for a couple of weeks; you're going to be there a long time.'" Eventually, though the two met up. "One thing led to another, and I worked as [Beck's] assistant for a number of years after that. ...

"I went up to the editors at Marvel a few times - I stayed at Mike Zeck's house; he was nice enough to put me up - and showed them my work. They told me that it was pretty good, but not quite there, so I went over to Charlton Comics and said, 'Look, I know that you're not publishing any new material. Why don't you publish some of *my* work instead of some of the reprints, for free, just so I can see what it looks like in print?' They agreed, and then figured that if *I* was so eager, there must be *other* guys out there willing to do [the same thing]. So *The Charlton Bullseye* was born."

Advice to aspiring creators:
"Over and over, the advice is always the same: Study your anatomy, study your perspective. There are a lot of good books out there on the basics of drawing. I find that a lot of people haven't done the basics.

"You have to take risks. It's difficult, because [artwork] is very personal. The only way to progress is to do it, to find out what you're doing wrong and correct it. ...

"I learned a lot from being in fanzines. I tried to get in print any way I could. I feel that in print, your work gets depersonalized, and you're able to see it *almost* as an outsider. It's difficult to be objective, but once you see your work next to your favorite artist's, it's easier to see where your mistakes are. So my advice is to get in print - *somehow.* There are all kinds of independent publishers out there today."

Scott Saavedra

Scott Saavedra has written and/or drawn for Fantagraphics, Disney, Mad Dog, Eclipse, and Marvel/Epic, but is likely best known for his creation Dr. Radium, Man of Science, *which has been published in various forms by Slave Labor for nearly a decade. His latest creation is the Slave Labor series* Java Town.

Date and place of birth:
February 4th, 1960; Los Angeles, California.

First exposure to comics:
"I don't exactly recall. I have a dim memory of a coverless 3D Batman comic - circa 1967 - that I found odd but compelling. A year or two later, a couple of neighbor pals showed me their collections of comics and *Mad* paperbacks.

"I still remember seeing my first *Mad* [book] - *Greasy Mad Stuff*. I couldn't *believe* what I was seeing and probably fell in love for the first time right then and there. Here was a world that I wanted to be a part of. I have been absolutely hooked ever since."

Breaking in:
"I got work assisting Joe Chiodo in coloring a couple of stories for Bruce Jones Associates/Pacific Comics. I met Joe through a mutual friend. Shortly after that, I met Slave Labor Graphics publisher Dan Vado through another mutual friend. He was looking for a new series to publish through his fledgling company, and experience wasn't a qualification. I took about a week to whip up sample pages for a comic called *It's Science with Dr. Radium* and Dan accepted the series.

"I got lucky. On my first try, not only did I find a publisher, I found an honorable one at that. We've worked together ever since."

Advice to aspiring creators:
"Live life. Find love. Draw. Write. Dream. Watch TV. Drink lots of coffee. Share your talents. No-one will ever know your gifts if you keep them hidden away."

David L. Seidman

David L. Seidman was a co-founder and senior editor at Disney Comics, editing such titles as Mickey Mouse Adventures, Walt Disney's Comics and Stories, *and* Roger Rabbit's Toontown. *He has written for Marvel Comics'* Disney Afternoon *and currently serves as marketing and promotions manager for Claypool Comics.*

Date and place of birth:
June 8th, 1958; Los Angeles, California.

First exposure to comics:
"A *Batman 80-Page Giant* published in the mid 1960s," David recalls. "It dealt with the strange lives of Batman, featuring such tales as 'Mayor Bruce Wayne' and - one of the weirdest titles in mainstream comics - 'Ride, Bat-Hombre, Ride!'. From then on, I was hooked."

Breaking in:
"It was a roundabout route," says David.

"I liked writing, so I became an English major when I went to college - UCLA, class of '80. As my senior year approached, with graduation and job-hunting to follow, I realized that I would have nothing but a college degree to put on my resumé - not exactly a strategic advantage in a job market flooded with new grads. I took two actions to build up my resumé: (1) I founded the campus' comic-book club to show prospective employers that I was a go-getter, and to meet girls. (It worked, too, but let's focus on the prospective employers.) (2) I secured unpaid editorial internships at local magazines.

"These activities would help break me into comics, although I didn't know it at the time.

"After graduation, I was a freelance journalist while looking for a full-time job as a writer. Among the articles that I sold were a review of science-fiction comics anthologies, which ran in *The Comics Journal*, and an analysis of the traits that would create a perfect superhero, which ran in *Amazing Heroes*.

"In early 1982, *The Los Angeles Times* ran a classified ad looking for someone who would, among other things, edit comic strips for *The Times*' syndicate. As one of very few candidates who knew both editing and comics, I got the job.

"At the 1982 San Diego Comic-Con, I met cartoonist Lee Nordling, who had a comic strip to sell. Lee happened to be president of the Comic Art Professionals Society, a group of local cartoonists. Months later, I called Lee - but not to buy his strip. My syndicate's art director was leaving, we needed a replacement, and I wanted a cartoonist in the job. I asked if Lee knew anyone suitable. He suggested himself and got the job.

"In 1986 - I think; memory gets hazy - Lee moved to Disney Publishing's Creative Services division. Creative Services oversaw all Disney publications and made certain that the characters were written and drawn properly.

"In 1988, Lee called *me*. He knew that I wanted to leave the syndicate, and he told me that Creative Services needed an editor to work on children's books and comic stories. I applied and got the job.

"In the spring of '89, the head of Creative Services called in staff cartoonist Bob Foster and me. Disney's licensed publisher for comics, Gladstone, was coming to the end of its contract term, and Disney wanted to bring the comics in-house. Bob and I, along with Len Wein, who was brought in shortly thereafter as editor-in-chief, became the founding editors of Disney Comics.

"And that's how I broke in."

Advice to aspiring creators:

"*Get in print*. Getting your work in print leads editors to believe that you're professional, or at least working to become professional. So take any opportunity. Work for free if you must - a number of freelancers have - but get in print.

"*Find out the publishers' guidelines for submission*. As an editor, I've often received submissions that were wildly inappropriate. When I edited newspaper strips, for example, I received submissions that were in a foreign language, that were pornographic, or that weren't comic strips at all. I turned them down. Call the company's editorial department and ask for the guidelines for submission - and follow them! They'll save you a lot of unnecessary rejection.

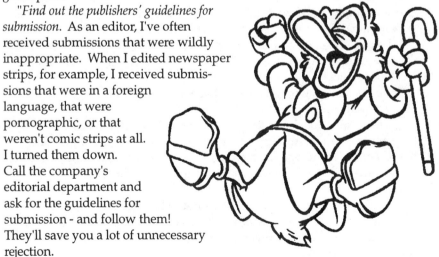

"*Be prepared*. When you go to a convention, keep copies of your work at hand. When you meet an editor who can give you [an assignment], you'll have the work handy for him to review on the spot or to take back to his office. On every page, put your name, address, and phone number.

"*Ask for referrals*. Let's say that you show your work to an editor, and he turns it down. Ask him if he knows of anyone who'd buy it. He may know an editor or a company that's open to working with new people. Use that information!

"*Do not fray an editor's nerves*. You'd be surprised at how many aspiring freelancers will nag an editor mercilessly or berate him, as if these actions will make the editor happy to work with them. There are better ways to influence an editor.

"If an editor says that your work is no good, then don't shout, 'You vaporhead! You don't know talent when you see it!' Instead, ask him what you should do to improve. Then take his advice and try him again.

"If his advice isn't clear, then ask him to clarify it.

"If his advice is clear but idiotic, then calmly and logically propose a better way to reach whatever goal he wants you to reach. Or find another editor.

"If he neglects you - editors are notoriously slow to return phone calls and answer submissions - then call him occasionally; once a month seems okay. And be polite.

"If he gives you work but treats you *so badly* that you have to walk off the job, then do it with calm maturity - even friendliness, if you can muster it.

"Good luck!"

Previous page: Scrooge McDuck, one of Carl Barks' classic Disney characters.

Don Simpson

Don Simpson's career began over a decade ago with Megaton Man, *a parody/ adventure series published by Kitchen Sink Press. Other work includes* Wendy Whitebread *for Fantagraphics Books' Eros imprint, contributions to DC Comics' innovative anthology* Wasteland, *and* Splittin' Image, The Savage Dragon vs. the Savage Megaton Man, The normalman/Megaton Man Special, *and* 1963 *for Image. He currently publishes* Bizarre Heroes, *a revival and expansion of many of his previous creations, through his own Fiasco Comics.*

Date and place of birth:
December 3rd, 1961; Garden City; Michigan.

First exposure to comics:
"My first exposure to comics was the Adam West *Batman* TV show in the late '60s, followed by the George Reeves *Superman* reruns, which led to the Sunday-funnies versions as well as the Saturday-morning animated versions. I remember getting coverless DC comics when visiting Santa Claus, but the Bizarros and Bat-Mites didn't hook me. I also recall various Marvel comics floating around, but didn't actually latch on 'til I was ten years old - the summer of 1972.

"I [then] knew immediately that I wanted to draw comics when I grew up, and read Marvels almost exclusively from 1972 to 1977. They dwindled off somewhat during high school, when I discovered *Heavy Metal*, undergrounds, Eisner *Spirit* reprints, and Wally Wood's *Cannon*. I fell under the influence of R. Crumb and the Europeans Moebius, Bilal, and Manara as well as *The Comics Journal* in the early '80s. I turned pro in 1984, and have since been studying the roots of American cartooning in comic strips and the Golden Age of comic books."

Breaking in:
"I met Marvel penciler Keith Pollard around 1977, as a sophomore in high school. I showed him my pencil samples, which I made using Marvel characters. Gradually, I decided to ink, script, and letter the samples as well, and, having gone that far, figured that I might as well use my own characters rather than Marvel's.

"I got myriad rejections from Marvel, *Heavy Metal*, and even Kitchen Sink. I took various odd jobs and commercial-art jobs, dropped out of art college, washed dishes in a restaurant. ...

"In 1983, I began work on a full-fledged comic. Luckily, I had the perfect character to hang all of my influences on - Megaton Man, a parody of over-muscled superheroes.

"[*Megaton Man*] was rejected by several publishers but picked up by Kitchen Sink Press for a ten-issue run. I have had a prosperous ten-year career creating my own comics as well as freelancing for just about every publisher. In 1994, I established my own publishing imprint, Fiasco Comics, in order to publish my ongoing comics series, *Bizarre Heroes*, an outgrowth of the 'universe' of characters that I created for Kitchen Sink. *BH* is my one focus from now on for new, creator-owned work. I also plan to reprint the Kitchen material, and offer bookshelf collections of my work."

Advice to aspiring creators:

"If you have drawing ability and are interested in cartooning, teach yourself the fundamentals of structure and figure drawing. Learn inking and lettering as well, for they will serve you in the years to come. Become familiar with computers, because that's where it's all heading. Learn to type. If you can read and write the English language, chances are that you can write a passable comics script, and you'll only get better, so start now. In short, do the whole thing - pencil-ing, inking, scripting, lettering, logo design, and coloring - just like me.

"What's important is what *you* have to offer. The world doesn't need any more *Hulk* or *Star Trek* stories. The world needs your original, distinctive, *insightful* stories. Bring your imagination to life on paper. No-one else can or will do that for you. Have faith in yourself, and concentrate on im-provement little by little. You've got a lifetime to get good at it, but you need to start now."

Right: Don Simpson's Megaton Man.

Evan Skolnick

Evan Skolnick worked on Marvel Comics' editorial staff for six years, lending his skills to such diverse titles as Alf, Bill and Ted's Excellent Comic Book, Marvel Year in Review, The Original Ghost Rider, Dr. Strange, *and* Ghost Rider 2099. *His writing credits include* William Shatner's TekWorld, RoboCop, Nova, *and, currently,* The New Warriors.

First exposure to comics:

"A lot of people who work in comics are die-hard fans - they know every comic book that they've ever read, they remember the *first* one, they remember issue numbers of things that happened fifteen, twenty years ago. I'm not like that.

"I *do* remember that I was a particular fan of Spider-Man when I was very young, reading some of the stuff in the '70s. But I honestly don't remember which [issues]. I was more into science fiction and *Star Trek* and that sort of thing. Before going to college, I worked at a 7-11, and I was able to read a lot of the comic books for free during my break. I really got into *Spider-Man* again, and *Daredevil*, and *The X-Men* - almost all of the Marvels."

Breaking in:

"I *thought* that I was going to go into journalism. When I was about fourteen, fifteen years old, I started a little magazine based on *Dungeons and Dragons*. So I knew that I wanted to be in publishing in some capacity. I've also always had an interest in design, and in art. I've never really had the drawing ability to be a professional artist, but when I went to college I studied English and journalism *and* graphic design. It's not easy to find a job where you can combine writing, design, art - *all* of those things - so comics was a really natural place to go to flex all of those muscles at once.

"My first freelance work at Marvel was coloring. It's not an uncommon thing for a struggling assistant editor working on a very low salary in publishing to want to get freelance [work], and coloring was something that almost anyone could do. The question was whether you could you do it *well*. My background helped me that way, because I'd had college courses in color theory and I felt that I could do it. Plus, Gregory Wright was my first editor when I was an assistant editor at Marvel, and he was a very prominent colorist. I learned a lot from Greg.

"So I got coloring work, and I found that I was fairly professional at it but that I actually didn't *like* coloring. As I would tell people, I liked *having colored* - when I was done, I was proud that it was a good job and I was glad that I did it. But the process was just excruciating, because it didn't come that naturally to me. Someone like Gregory Wright, he looks at a page and he immediately can conceive of what it should be. I have to struggle with every color. I did color a lot of covers in my days as an editor; I enjoyed that because I could do the whole thing in less than an hour or so. ...

"My first entrance into professional comics at all was on staff at Marvel, so my freelance had to be for Marvel, because when you're on staff at one [publisher] you can't really freelance for another. I was an assistant editor, I wanted to write, I felt *ready* to write - I actually *wasn't*, but I felt that I *was*, and I certainly wanted to take a crack at it."

Advice to aspiring creators:

"If you're new, writing is absolutely the hardest [area] to break into: If you're a new artist, you can show your stuff and an editor can tell within seconds whether you have talent, whether you have potential. A writer cannot give [an editor] that information in a few seconds; you need to read a lot of stuff by that writer to see if he knows what he's doing, and most editors don't have time for that - they go for people who've already established themselves as writers, so they know what they're getting. Editors generally don't have time to teach writers the format, the many things that go into writing a comic book.

"If you're on the outside, and you have not written anything for comics at all, you have literally zero chance of getting writing work [at Marvel]. That's a basic fact. Editors just don't have time to even [consider] you unless you've written before - it's that old Catch-22. Now, being on the inside as, say, an assistant editor, which is where most people want to start writing at Marvel, it *is* easier to get little jobs here and there. The editors know you, you know them. But it's by

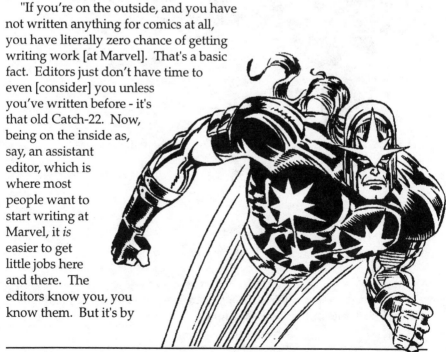

no means *assumed* - you still have to bust your hump to get [an assignment]. Your first job is by far the hardest to get, because once you've got your first one, you can say, "Well, I did this over here. Can I do something for *you?*" And you can parlay the work that you've done into *more* work and as editors find that you've done more work, they're more likely to trust that you know how to do this.

"Sure, there are times when editors at *any* company will hire their buddies whether or not their buddies are any good; however, my experience is that editors and assistant editors on staff at Marvel get work partly because they're there, because the editors know who they are, and partly because they're *editors* - you figure that if an editor can edit, he probably knows something about writing. It took me quite a while. Getting *New Warriors* took a very long time."

Above and previous page: Speedball and Nova, two characters whose lives Evan Skolnick chronicles in The New Warriors.

Tom Sniegoski

Tom Sniegoski is the longtime writer of Vengeance of Vampirella *for Harris Comics, and recently revived* The Rook *for the same publisher.*

Date and place of birth:
February 4th, 1962; somewhere in Massachusetts.

First exposure to comics:
"I probably have been a comic-book fan right from the start, from when I was very little, but I started really *collecting* them in about third or fourth grade," Tom says. As far as awareness of the writers and artists behind the stories, though, "that probably didn't happen until junior high school - the Stan Lee and Jack Kirby *Fantastic Fours*, because Marvel always had that attitude where you were part of the gang : 'Come on in! It's the Merry Marvel Marching Society!', and all that stuff. ...

"I always had a kind of creative spark, dabbling in drawing as well as writing. I had a lot of friends who were more talented than I was who actually *did* their own comics; they drew them and stapled them together - the whole nine yards. But I didn't sit down in sixth grade or whatever and say, 'I'm gonna write comics.' That was like being a movie star or an astronaut - it had a godlike status. 'I'm never gonna do *that*.'"

Breaking in:
"It's funny, because through high school I'd done yearbook illustrations and that sort of thing, and I always thought that I was going to head towards some kind of an art career. Then all of a sudden I took a side street and headed into the writing aspect. I was writing pretty regularly for awhile, and thought that I might like to have a career as a novelist or as a short-story writer. I was still buying comics religiously, but I never thought that my writing talent could be applied to that. ...

Tom made the crossover from prose to comics when he met Steve Bissette, the former artist on DC's *Swamp Thing* who had begun publishing the horror-comics anthology *Taboo*. Bissette, says Tom, "had read one of my short stories and said, 'We'd love to do this as an adaptation in *Taboo*.' And all of a sudden, the light dawned - 'I could write comic books'' So I adapted the story with an artist named Mike Hoffman. Scripting was some kind of arcane thing that nobody had really taught me how to do, so it was hit-or-miss for me. Mike was really neat to work with; he said, 'Give me [your script] and I'll add what I know and we'll come up with something nice.' And that's pretty much what happened.

"[*Taboo*] was a great foot in the door. I gained new respect when I could say I that worked with Steve Bissette on *Taboo*. That's one advantage that I had over somebody else trying to get a gig with an independent company. If I didn't have the *Taboo* thing, I don't know that people would've listened. It's like having a good resumé."

How did Tom fall in with Harris Comics? "Again it involves Steve Bissette, who's been like my guardian," he laughs. "I was talking to him at a New York [convention] about wacky movies or something like that and Meloney Crawford-Chadwick, who was the big chief at Harris, came up *quickly* to the table, almost as if she wanted to finish a conversation that they'd been having earlier, but had to go. I didn't want to intrude on their conversation, so I started to leave, and as I started to leave, Steve grabbed my shirt sleeve and pulled me back and said, 'Meloney, this is Tom Sniegoski; he's written for *Taboo* and he's done some independent books and stuff, and he's really good.' Meloney flipped me a card and said, 'We're doing a revival of a lot of the old Warren stuff. Why don't you give me a call if you get any ideas?' I gave her a call two days after that, and within a few weeks I had a couple of proposals for other series. And then came the offer of *Vampirella*. Steve's words were enough to get someone to say, '*Steve* thinks he's good…'"

Advice to aspiring creators:
"Perseverance. Don'tfeel that you're never gonna make it. If you want to do it, just keep plugging away. If you have the talent, and it's just that your stuff hasn't been given the opportunity, your opportunity will come if you persevere."

Frank Thorne

Frank Thorne will always be the definitive artist of Marvel Comics' Red Sonja, based on the Robert E. Howard character, but his long career also includes work on Tomahawk *and* Korak *for DC,* The Mighty Samson *for Gold Key, the miniseries* Ribit *at Comico, and his own* Moonshine McJuggs *for Playboy. Fantagraphics Books has published a multi-volume set titled* The Erotic Worlds of Frank Thorne *showcasing some of the artist's own favorite work.*

Date and place of birth:
   June 16th, 1930; Rahway, New Jersey.

First exposure to comics:
   "Reading Captain Marvel, the Atom, and the turning point - Sheena, Queen of the Jungle."

Breaking in:
   "Joe Archibald, the splendid editor at Standard Comics, gave me my first assignment in 1948 - an eight-pager for *Intimate Love*."

Advice to aspiring creators:
   "Strive to create and own your material. Comics by committee do not interest me. Write, draw, letter, and color your stuff. The best and only solid things that intrigue me are the creations done completely by the hand of the sole creator. Yes, you *can* tell when the statement is authored by a single hand.
   "If you're planning to go into this craft for money, forget it - work for the Post Office.
   "In matters of the creative process, please yourself first."

Left: Frank Thorne's Ribit.

Jim Valentino

Jim Valentino is a co-founder of Image Comics. He is the creator of ShadowHawk *and other Image series, many of which he has written and/or drawn, and of* normalman, *an affectionate satire of comics past published variously by Aardvark-Vanaheim, Renegade, and Slave Labor. He once wrote and drew Marvel's* Guardians of the Galaxy.

Date and place of birth:
October 28th, 1952; Bronx, New York.

First exposure to comics:
"Hard to say - probably when I was three or four. My father, who enjoyed comics during World War II, first brought them to my attention when he realized that the drawings that I was making were very cartoon-like."

Breaking in:
"Inspired by a local San Diego cartoonist, Joel Milke, I took my work to a quick-copy printer and had two hundred copies of a book, *Christmas Comics*, printed. From there I joined a network of other small-press publishers and came to the attention of Dave and Deni Sim [then co-publishers of Aardvark-Vanaheim], thanks to the intervention of a friend, Clay Geerdes. Dave and Deni published *normalman* and, later, *Valentino*. To break into mainstream comics, I sent samples to various editors on a weekly basis - rotating the lucky recipients and collecting rejection slips."

Advice to aspiring creators:
• "Learn your craft *first*. Study. As starting points, I suggest *The Complete Guide to Drawing from Life* by George Brigman for gestures, *Comics and Sequential Art* by Will Eisner for storytelling, and *Understanding Comics* by Scott McCloud for underlying philosophy of the form. The biggest mistake that I see [among aspiring creators] is that artists have failed to learn their craft. Underdrawing, composition, and gesture usually suffer the most, but basic disciplines such as perspective and anatomy are often absent as well.

- "Tenacity pays off. Do plenty of samples, and send them everywhere. A rejection slip does not mean that [editors] don't like you. It just means that your work needs to improve.

- "Judge your work harshly. Put pages away and don't look at them until you've done ten more. Take your work to conventions and *listen* to the criticisms that you get. If you keep hearing the same complaint over and over, be assured that there isn't a conspiracy on [the reviewers'] part, but a weakness on yours. Define your weaknesses and work to strengthen them.

- "Network. Get to know people. Let them get to know you. Developing positive relationships can only work to your advantage. *No-one* wants to work with an argumentative, overly defensive newcomer - trust me! Take your ego and bury it; there are far too many primadonnas in this business as it is.

- "Don't fall into the trap that you *must* be a penciler to be a 'star'. There is a desperate need for good inkers, letterers, colorists, and, yes, *writers* out there. Find a niche, fill a need. Be tenacious. Work hard.

- "Don't give up. If this is what you want, then don't let *anyone* talk you out of it."

Previous page: Jim Valentino's beloved creation normalman.

Kate Van Zyl
Joyce Slaton

Kate Van Zyl publishes Manic Panic *under the Plump Not Pregnant Comix label and distributes issues through record stores and other alternative outlets in the Florida area. Joyce Slaton is the head writer for* Manic Panic *and a former reporter for* Sassy; *she self-publishes the 'zine* Lardass, *which is about whatever she wants.*

Date and place of birth:
Kate: November 11th, 1970; Orlando, Florida.
Joyce: August 8th, 1970; somewhere in Tennessee.

First exposure to comics:
Kate: "I was a big fan of *Love and Rockets,* and *Archie,* and *Mad.* Not the violent stuff, the *real* stuff - at least, as far as *I'm* concerned, it's real."
Joyce: Joyce is not a big comics reader, but she likes Peter Bagge's *Bradleys* stories.

Breaking in:
Kate: "I was hanging out with some friends, and I got introduced to two guys who ended up working for Revolutionary. They were doing their own thing, and they saw that I could draw halfway decently, and they saw that I had a really good sense of humor - a really sick, twisted sense of humor, actually - and they figured that I could draw for *them*. When I decided that what I *really* wanted to do was just too bizarre for anybody else to do but me, and maybe my friend Joyce, then I just did it myself. I wanted to do stuff that had never been seen before. The [comics] audience is made up of thirteen-year-old boys; I don't see many *girls* - I don't think that there's anything out there for them to read."
Joyce: "There's not that many comics out there that women like. And there's a *reason* why most comics

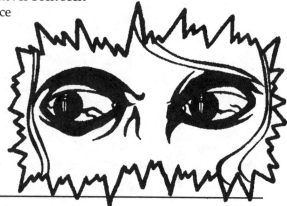

buyers are men: Women generally don't like super-heroes and don't like women being pictured as huge-breasted Amazons; it's offensive and degrading to women - it is to *me*, anyway. So we want to create comics for men *and* women, about real people, that aren't so formulaic, as most of the superhero comics tend to be. And we've gotten a pretty big response, let me tell you."

Advice to aspiring creators:

Kate: "As a penciler, keep drawing, no matter what happens. All you need is paper and a pencil. You can use computers, you can use all the tricks in the world, but all you *need* is paper and a pencil and you're getting across an idea through illustration, and that's what comics *is*."

Joyce: "I'm coming at it more from a writing point of view. I do my 'zine, I'm a reporter, I just write, write, write, write, write like a fiend. …

Joyce: "Xeroxing is very inexpensive. How much did you end up paying, Kate? Thirty dollars for a hundred issues. Thirty dollars! And she's already made her money back. Self-publishing [minicomics] is an extremely wonderful option; it's easy, and it's good for people who are doing things out of the mainstream. *Anybody* can do it. And no matter how weird your stuff is, *somebody* is going to like it. If you're looking around, and you don't see anything out there that you like, that means that there's a gap in the market that's not being filled, so you should step right in there."

Above and previous page: Artwork from Kate Van Zyl's Manic Panic.

Wayne Vansant

Wayne Vansant is an accomplished creator in the war-comics genre, with credits in Marvel's The 'Nam *and* Semper Fi, *Apple's* Days of Wrath, *Dark Horse's* Medal of Honor, *and Eclipse's* Real War Stories.

Date and place of birth:
   July 13th, 1949; Atlanta, Georgia.

First exposure to comics:
   "I actually drew comics before I saw them," Wayne says. Isnpired by such films as *20,000 Leagues under the Sea* and the *Flash Gordon* serials, he would draw his own versions on paper. "I started *reading* comics later, at about the age of six of seven - mostly Disneys," he recalls.

Breaking in:
   "When *Savage Tales* came out - the second series - I sent a letter to editor Larry Hama with some artwork and story ideas and he responded with a positive letter back. That's it."

Advice to aspiring creators:
   "Artists: Learn to draw from life, *not* from comics. Being able to draw only like the hot artist of the day limits you, and tastes change. There is a big world outside of comic books.
   "Writers: Read! Read everything and anything. What comics today lack is *true* human emotion. And that is really what writing is all about."

Neil Vokes

Neil Vokes has worked with a variety of publishers throughout his career, penciling Robotech Masters *for Comico,* Blood of Dracula *for Apple,* Tarzan the Warrior *for Malibu,* Congorilla *for DC,* Jonny Demon *for Dark Horse, and the proverbial much, much more. Recent or upcoming projects include DC's adaptation of Douglas Adams' novel* Life, the Universe, and Everything, *Image's* Marvin, *and Claypool's* Elvira *and* Soulsearchers and Company.

Date and place of birth:
   May 12th, 1954; Ft. Lauderdale, Florida.

First exposure to comics:
   "My father said that I was about four when I started reading comics. They helped me learn how to read. Of course, he also *destroyed* my comics as I got older. They would warp my mind, you know. (Hmm... Maybe he was right!)
   "The first comics that I remember were Superman comics. I used to read them at the barber shop next door or buy them at the corner drugstore. Speculators beware: I would buy my books, scan them, then roll them up, so I could carry them in my back pocket. Believe it or not, we used to *read* comic books thirty years ago, for entertainment!!

"As I got older, I started doodling a little. My first heroes were Curt Swan, Kirby, Ditko, and some others. ... I also watched a lot of movies, because my dad was a movie fan. I watched tons and tons of movies. And that helped my drawing - it gave me a certain visual sense. I wasn't necessarily a good artist at the time, but I had an idea how to visually tell stories."

Breaking in:

"I was twenty-nine. I'd met a friend of mine, Rich Rankin, at a comics shop. We got together and talked about trying to break into the business, but we didn't know how, so we decided to do some samples. He inked my pencils, and we were going to turn around and do the opposite, where I would ink something of *his*, but as it turned out we didn't need to go any further: I was the penciler and he was the inker.

"We sent the samples to various companies. Comico was just gearing up around then, so we met with [the publishers] and became friends with the guys. We did a couple of issues of a book that never got published, called *Az*, which gave me some training. Then Comico acquired the *Robotech* stuff, and gave us a choice of whichever of those books we wanted to do. We chose *Masters*. We got the job mostly because we worked hard, we were on deadline. That was 1983. I've been working ever since.

"By the way, I'd like to add that I wouldn't have even made the first step into comics without my wife Siri's help. She encouraged and supported me, both financially and emotionally."

Advice for aspiring creators:

"If you want to get into the business, you have to love doing it. Drawing - and I'm sure writing is very much the same - is a passionate kind of job. You're taking so much from inside.

"You have to learn how to discipline yourself, as I discovered my first few years. I ended up very close to a nervous breakdown, because I didn't know how to discipline my time; I'd work really, really hard up to the last few days of a deadline, and then I'd pass out for a few days. I learned how to control that.

"There's no magic way of doing it. A lot of it is luck - Rich and I were in the right place at the right time. Work hard, keep at it. You have to do it constantly, every day. Every time you've drawn a picture, you've learned a little bit more about your work.

"You'll probably get a lot of disappointments, a lot of rejections, and when the next 'glut doomsday' comes, a lot of people won't get much work. It's good to start *anywhere* - get into whatever company there is. Small companies, large companies, whoever'll take you. Whatever it is, it's *experience*. I worked for all the companies, up and down; I still, now, do work for small, independent companies because I get a kick out of doing that. And I like to draw."

Previous page: A Neil Vokes-drawn panel from the Teenage Mutant Ninja Turtles/Flaming Carrot *crossover.*

Mark Waid

Mark Waid, Ex-Boy Editor, helmed the Fantagraphics fanzine Amazing Heroes *and such DC series as* The Legion of Super-Heroes, Secret Origins, *and* Doom Patrol. *His writing credits include* Flash, Impulse, Valor, *and* Legionnaires *for DC;* Veronica *and* Riverdale High *for Archie; and* Captain America, Deadpool, *and* X-Men *for Marvel. He's currently at work the much anticipated DC mini-series* Kingdom Come *with Alex Ross.*

Date and place of birth:
March 21st, 1962; Hueytown, Alabama.

First exposure to comics:
"*Batman* #180, in 1966. My father bought it for me at the very beginning of the Batmania craze that swept the late '60s. I started reading [comics] then and never stopped, not even after I discovered girls."

Breaking in:
"Something that I learned early on is that editors don't hire plot synopses - they hire *people*. Getting to know comics pros and editors by working at local conventions created a lot of opportunities for me and opened a lot of doors. Once I began writing for the fan press - *Amazing Heroes, Comics Buyer's Guide*, those sorts of publications - I was able to keep those doors open by maintaining contacts.

The fact that [former DC editor] Julie Schwartz recognized my name from my coverage of *Ambush Bug* was absolutely the only thing that allowed me passage into his office one afternoon - and allowed me to sell him my very first story, an eight-page Superman job for *Action Comics*.

"In time, networking through the fan press netted me an editorial job at DC. I left that position three years later, but not before establishing personal contacts that serve me to this day."

Advice to aspiring creators:
"Get an editorial job at DC. Okay, not really… But one way or another, find a way to meet editors personally, whether through appointments or conventions. Be polite and pleasant under all circumstances; in this industry, you never know for sure that the powerless-jerk assistant editor on *Yawnman* won't be running the company five years from now and determining your fate with a gesture.

"Whether writer or artist, never in a gajillion years brag that you could do the job 'better than the guy who's on the book now'. Congratulations! You've just insulted the personal taste of the editor who hired him in the first place! Nice goin', Ace.

"Artists: Always present samples that tell a story. One way to hone your storytelling skills is to lob your pal - or your brother or your mom - a copy of a comic pencilled by someone with plenty of experience - Sal Buscema, John Romita Jr., John Byrne, whoever has an established rep. Make sure that it's a comic that you haven't yourself seen. Have your pal jot down a few paragraphs describing the action on several pages. Ta-dah! Instant plot! Pencil it out, then compare it to what was published. Take note of how the Experienced Pro interpreted the plot, and contrast it with your own pencils for a learning experience.

"Writers: Write the kinds of stories that *you'd* like to read. Don't settle for grudgingly hacking out Image knock-offs, babes-with-swords stories, or whatever other sub-genre might be 'hot' this month. If you approach your stories without a true love for the subject matter, you're doomed. Stories born of a cynical attempt to copy current market trends glow like plutonium. No-one's going to really get into your work if you don't have something fresh and original to say. Sure, you might stumble into a few assignments and eke out a living with your *Youngblood* rip-off that all your friends think is the *best*, but if you can't razzle and dazzle *strangers* with new ideas, new themes, and new things to say, you'll be colder than the flip side of a pillow in no time. Above all, be innovative, not imitative."

Previous page: Mark Waid's co-creation Impulse, penciled by Humberto Ramos and inked by Wayne Faucher.

Shannon Wheeler

Shannon Wheeler is the creator of Too Much Coffee Man, *which is self-syndi-cated to various newspapers and 'zines around the country and published in comic-book form by Adhesive Comics, a publishing collective of which Shannon is a founding member.*

First exposure to comics:
"I remember buying Marvel horror comics back when they were fifteen cents each. I really liked horror movies, and my enthusiasm poured over into the comics. Soon I found sci-fi comics, and eventually superheroes."

Breaking in:
"I don't know that I *have* broken in. I tried to find publishers when I first started drawing comics, but I didn't meet with much success. Some friends and I founded a small company to publish our own material; we started with an anthology, *Jab*, and eventually moved to publishing independent titles."

Advice to aspiring creators:
"Start small and finish your projects. It's frustrating seeing people with sets of characters but no stories, or stories and no art. I've found it to be a do-it-yourself industry: If you want it published, publish it. If you want it drawn, draw it. When you finally don't need offers, you'll get them."

Above: An eternal question posed by Shannon Wheeler's Too Much Coffee Man.

Jim Woodring

Jim Woodring is the co-creator of Tantalizing Stories *and the creator, writer, and artist behind Fantagraphics'* Jim *and* Tundra's *Frank in the River. He also wrote the* Aliens: Labyrinth *mini-series for Dark Horse.*

Date and place of birth:
October 11th, 1952; Los Angeles, California.

First exposure to comics:
"Reading *Nancy* in the LA *Times*, age four. I remember being disturbed that my father thought that *Nancy* was stupid."

Breaking in:

"At age twenty, my friend John Dorman and I made up portfolios of our work and took 'em to Petersen Publishing, where *Car-Toons* was edited by Dennis Ellefson. We both got assignments. It was a big day for us, I can tell you."

Advice to aspiring creators:
"Unless you're already rich, learn to live inexpensively. Put off having a family until you're a steadily working pro. Devote yourself to the perfection of your craft. Consider yourself an *artist*. Be humble despite your high self-regard. Swipe to learn, but never for your finished work. Develop your own style. Get plenty of exercise."

Above: Jim Woodring's Frank.

Phil Yeh

Phil Yeh is the creator and publisher of Frank the Unicorn, Penguin and Pencilguin, The Winged Tiger, *and many other comic books and graphic novels. Phil is also the founder of Cartoonists across America (now Cartoonists across the World), an organization that is promoting literacy, creativity, and other positive issues on a fifteen-year global tour. Among Phil's numerous awards and honors is a postage stamp issued in Hungary in 1990 using his artwork to celebrate the International Year of Literacy. He is currently working with his partner, Ted Lai, on various live-action and animated film projects and interactive CD-ROM versions of his comics.*

Date and place of birth:
October 7th, 1953; Chicago, Illinois.

First exposure to comics:
"I bought my first comic book, an issue of *Batman*, at the age of ten on a family vacation," Phil remembers. "My sisters and brother had a few copies of *Dennis the Menace* and *Archie* along on that trip as well.

"We didn't have comic books in our home for the most part. My parents frowned on them. They encouraged us to read 'real' books and to listen to good music and go to museums and play outside; I have come to appreciate their good taste and common sense. I spent most of my youth reading anything *but* comic books. I read adventure books, books about baseball, Ray Bradbury and HG Wells, and lots of biographies about anyone. I still love to read biographies!

"I later had a chance to see some old comic books belonging to an older neighbor who also collected science fiction. My first loves were *Tintin*, *Sugar and Spike*, and Jack Cole's *Plastic Man*. I really only collected comic books for about two years from the ages of fourteen to sixteen after a friend came over and gave me about four-hundred DC comics. The same friend would bring me new issues each week to keep 'my' collection up to date. I enjoyed a few superhero comics during that time - the late '60s - like *The Flash*, *The Legion of Super-Heroes*, and [Neal] Adams and [Denny] O'Neil's *Green Lantern/Green Arrow*. But my favorite comic book was still Sheldon Mayer's *Sugar and Spike*. I also loved Stan Lynde's *Rick O'Shay* and Dick Moore's *Gasoline Alley* in the daily newspapers, and I still read *Tintin* and *Asterix*."

Breaking in:

"My father *did* point out the good cartoonists in the newspaper. He had a good eye for quality drawing. My dad was an engineer, but he drew little flip books for me when I was very young, and by the time I was five I was making up my own little cartoon books.

"When I was fourteen years old, I briefly thought that I wanted to work for DC Comics drawing superheroes. I actually sold them a gag that they used for a promotional piece. I still remember the excitement of getting a check for five dollars from National Periodical Publications [DC's former corporate identity] at the age of fourteen! All of my friends who loved comic books thought that I would someday be drawing *Superman* or *Batman*.

"The truth is that most of the mainstream comic books even *then* weren't really that good - and sadly, they are much worse today, with a few notable exceptions. I gave up collecting comic books and decided that I wanted to become a filmmaker. I had started making small movies with my father's eight-millimeter camera for class projects. Film and comics shared many of the same elements, but film was far more socially acceptable in American society.

"As my small movie projects grew in scope during high school, I discovered underground comic books when a friend of mine in art class brought in a copy of *Zap Comix*. I fell in love with Rick Griffin's beautiful black-and-white drawings the minute that I laid eyes on them. The freedom that these underground cartoonists had inspired me to become a professional artist [as well as] a filmmaker. These artists demonstrated that the medium of comics could tell any story in any style without the tired clichés of caped heroes and goofy plots.

"The underground artists also inspired me to go to San Francisco to actually *meet* these people. You could fly to San Francisco for about thirty dollars round-trip from Los Angeles when I was sixteen. My friends Paul Swain and Mark Eliot and I were like Dorothy in *The Wizard of Oz* on that first trip! We didn't have a clue about the city and in fact ended up walking miles and miles getting to know the city block by block. We met Gilbert

Shelton of *The Fabulous Furry Freak Brothers* on that trip, and Last Gasp publisher Ron Turner. Ron started me off on my underground collection the same way that my junior-high-school friend had started me off on my DC collection. Mark and I told Ron that we wanted to be professional artists and he just gave us as many comics as we wanted for *free*!

"We started our own little magazine in 1970 called *Cement*. It was filled with our attempts at underground comics. This was the beginning of more than two decades of publishing my own books, other people's books, and almost one hundred issues of *Uncle Jam*, a free alternative newspaper that ran from 1973 to 1991, filled with comics and interviews with many of my own favorite creators.

"I'm not sure that there was a time when I actually broke into 'professional' cartooning. When you publish your own work, you don't *have* to 'break in'. I was lucky enough to just *do* it and I have continued to be lucky enough to earn my living from my artwork since that time with only two very brief 'real' jobs in the last twenty-five years. And I still don't draw superheroes!"

Advice to aspiring creators:
"I speak to thousands of students all over the country every year through my Cartoonists across America literacy campaign, and I offer two words of advice to anyone who wants to get involved with any of the arts: 'Marry well.' I speak from experience here.

"The other piece of advice that I offer anyone is to be prepared to work your butt off for your art. I mentioned earlier that I was lucky enough to make my living as an artist for the majority of my life. Luck is really a small part of the picture. The truth is that I work sixteen to twenty hours a day on my art because I love to write, draw, paint, and create. I have three sons - ages fifteen, thirteen, and eleven- and they all want to be artists. I drill into their heads that they will have to work twice as hard as most people to be successful.

"I tell all young artists to draw from life - don't copy those goofy superheroes in comic books; draw real people and real buildings - and I tell young people to read 'real' books, and go to museums and travel and listen to good music and eat their vegetables. And my kids tell me that I'm an old man now, although we cartoonists never really grow up. Ask our wives or husbands.

"Comics is the easiest and least expensive art form to get into. Anyone can self-publish at the local copy shop, and black-and-white comic books don't cost that much to print. Remember those Ninja Turtles? I encourage *everyone* to tell their own stories. The most important thing about comics is that you should have a story to tell. If more people made their own comics, then I am convinced that more people would read comics *and* read 'real' books, too. Our literacy crisis would be over tomorrow if everyone would start drawing and writing their own comics! We'd also have a lot more variety in the comics shop.

"The last piece of advice that I have for aspiring creators is to get over their shyness and get out there and go to comic-book conventions and meet professional artists and other people with the same interests. Comics is part of show business, and the basic rule of show business is that talent counts but it also helps to know the right people. Make friends with everyone and don't be afraid of being the assistant to an older artist so that you can really learn something. There really is wisdom in age - I believed this when I was sixteen, and I *knew* it at forty.

"Don Rico, Hal Robinson, Favia, Sergio Aragonés, Alfredo Alcala, Dave Thorne, Jean Giraud (Moebius), and many other artists and writers gave me some really great advice over the years - and their friendship as well. I have been blessed to be able to meet so many talented people from all walks of life who have shared their wisdom with me. I have also been blessed with great partners - who are also my dear friends - who have helped me keep the business side under control all these years.

"Don't be afraid of your dreams. Turn off the TV and the video games and chain yourself to the drawing board. If you don't draw and you want to make comics: The industry always needs good writers. You become a great cartoonist by working hard - that's the big secret. The competition is pretty light these days, because many people living in the United States of America just don't have the discipline to really work this hard in the arts. We have a generation that wants instant results with the push of a remote. But if you are disciplined you can really go far."

Right and two pages prior: Phil Yeh artwork from Frank the Unicorn *and* Penguin & Pencilguin, *the latter co-written by Leigh Rubin.*

Ray Zone

Ray Zone has been bringing flat comics art into the third dimension for more than a decade. His work can be seen on DC's Batman 3D, *Eclipse's* Mr. Monster 3D, *Renegade's* normalman 3D Annual, *and numerous publications from his own 3D Zone.*

Date and place of birth:
   May 16th, 1947; Cleveland, Ohio.

First exposure to comics:
   "*Third Dimension Comics*, featuring Mighty Mouse. It was October, 1953. I was six."

Breaking in:
   Ray entered the professional comics sphere writing articles for fanzines. He came to write *Battle for a 3D World*, illustrated by Jack Kirby, and has since produced or published more than one-hundred 3D comic books.

Advice to aspiring creators:
   "Pursue your dream relentlessly," says Ray. "Never give up and you *will* succeed!"

THERE, NOW! ISN'T THAT BETTER?

Right: Ray Zone as seen by Jim Engel.

And, since fair is fair...

Brian Saner-Lamken

Brian Saner-Lamken is responsible for the book that you're reading right now. As a journalist and cartoonist, he has contributed to such industry publications as Comics Buyer's Guide, indy, *and* Comics Pro Magazine. *He is currently at work self-publishing a variety of minicomics through Boardwalk Press.*

Date and place of birth:
October 14th, 1970; Philadelphia, Pennsylvania.

First exposure to comics:
"My parents taught me to read at a very young age, and, to their credit, when I graduated from Dr. Seuss to *Dr. Strange* they kept on encouraging me rather than complaining that I preferred *comic* books to so-called *'real'* ones. In time, my love for comics - and especially superhero comics - led to an affection for literature and art of all kinds.

"I wish that I could remember my very first comic book, but I don't. My childhood favorites ran the gamut from the revival of the original Captain Marvel in DC's *Shazam* to his modern-day namesake over at Marvel. I had a special fondness for the *100-Page Super Spectaculars* that DC produced, crammed with great features and reprint material that opened a doorway to other eras."

Breaking in:
"When I was eight years old, I attended my first comic-book convention, and, with my mother next to me for moral support, I handed Jim Shooter - then editor-in-chief of Marvel Comics - some homemade comic books of mine to review. He asked if he could take them home to read at his leisure, and in a few weeks returned them with a very personal letter encouraging me to follow my dream.

"A good ten years later, during a trip home from college, it dawned on me that I just wasn't going to shake this comics thing, and that if I really wanted to make a go of it, there was no time like the present: I'd rather have tried and failed early on than forever be wondering, 'What if...?' I redoubled my efforts at cartooning for the school newspaper, began seriously learning about the craft through every possible opportunity - earning academic credit at the same time when I could - and set out to meet as many professionals as possible to get some first-hand information. I wasn't expecting miracles overnight, but I now had a mission in life.

"By the beginning of my junior year, I'd sold my first article to *Comics Buyer's Guide*, and I felt secure - perhaps naively so - that if I couldn't get a 'creative' job in the industry, journalism would be happy to have me. Correspondence with numerous comics professionals, including the late Neal Pozner - at the time, DC Comics' new-talent liaison - provided me with a sort of 'graduate program' of my own making. At this point, I have yet to land a job writing a monthly title for one of the big-deal companies, but I've learned a lot about the business, I've learned a lot about *myself*, and I'm active and working in and around the industry that has given me a lifetime of joy. I've also come to realize more and more that there's a lot to be said for initiative; I'm quite capable of producing comics that are purely of my hands from start to finish, and if it falls to me to shepherd my creations to the waiting world, outisde the traditional channels, that's just fine. This book is a by-product of that perspective, and I think that it turned out pretty well."

Advice to aspiring creators:

"The thought of jumping in with my two cents now, knowing that you've read the advice of dozens of talented writers, artists, editors, and publishers on the pages preceding this, has me silently screaming 'Head for the appendices! I'm not worthy!' But I can't do any less than I asked of my contributors, so strap yourselves in.

"First, think long and hard about whether you do, indeed, want to make a living in the comics field and what exactly that means for you. It's not likely to be quick or easy, and you may end up with a bruised ego and lots of self-directed anger at spending so much time trying to get somewhere in this cockamamie biz when you could've gotten a teaching certificate, gone to medical school, or become a professional itinerant abroad. If, however, it doesn't matter, you want to do comics, you *need* to do comics, you're dedicated to your vision and nobody's gonna stop you, then *go forth and do*. You're just the kind of person whose work I want to read.

"There are, in fact, many ways to gain experience without committing yourself wholly and fully to becoming a comics professional, though the

---

time will come to take that leap. If you're in school, by all means, write and draw that comic strip for the school newspaper or magazine. Learn about your own perfectionism, others' expectations, and the 'good-or-Tuesday' compromise that comes from working under deadlines. Take on odd jobs or simply devote parts of your weekly schedule - your daily schedule, if you can - to making comics: Devise stories, sketch characters and settings, and above all *work toward a finished product*. Set a realistic goal and achieve it, then up the ante and do it again. Also, if you perceive yourself as 'only' a writer or 'only' an artist, hook up with someone else and learn about collaboration.

"As others have noted, it's essential to read and study more than comic books, but it's just as essential to read and study comic books more closely than may feel natural. Students of film watch movies with a very different eye than the casual viewer; students of comics need to do the same - to examine *why* their favorite stories are their favorites, *what* devices the writer and/or artist is using to create excitement, tension, suspense, dimension, pacing, reader identification, and all those wonderful things. Such dissection will likely lower your tolerance for bad comic books considerably, but that's not such bad news. And the better news is that - based on my own experience, at least - you'll still be able to read a *good* comic book like it's the freshest, newest thing in the world.

"Money is a very real concern for most people, and you probably won't have the luxury of exiting high school or college into your own personal studio to toil away every waking hour in pursuit of a job in the comics field. So do one of two things: Get a job that gives you minimal hassles and maximum time for your comics work, or get a job - or jobs - that will in some way hone your comics-creating skills.

"It's also a good idea to cultivate a close relationship with the people at your local comics shop. First, they're most likely to know of other aspiring or working professionals in the area for you to contact; second, if and when you choose to publish and distribute your own material, on a large or small scale, it's nice to have that hometown store in your corner.

"Last and most importantly, *don't give up*. You may need to shift priorities and rethink objectives based on financial or even emotional considerations, but keep plugging away and you *will* do it. Is luck a factor? Sure it is, for both good and bad. But talent and determination count for a lot in this world, too.

"Thanks for listening."

Previous page: The first pulse-pounding meeting of Brian Saner-Lamken's Shaboogie *and Stefan Blitz's* Technoboy. *Two pages prior: Artwork from Brian's minicomic* Falling.

Appendix A
Making Minicomics
by Matt Feazell

Editor's note: Matt Feazell, dean of the minicomics scene, responded to my plea for an appendix with his usual generosity by sending along the following essay. It originally appeared in minicomics form, but has been adapted and reformatted for ease of reading below; readers who would like to cut, fold, and staple a sample copy for reference and future enjoyment can obtain the original, uncut minicomic version by sending their address and a 55¢ stamp to Boardwalk Press at PO Box 362, Wynnewood, PA 19096, or through Matt Feazell's own Not Available Comics at the address found in the Resources section at the end of this book.

Every minicomic is made from a single sheet of paper printed on both sides then cut, folded, and stapled to make an eight-page booklet. This essay originally appeared in the form of a dummy book to show you how the pages should look when you take them to a printer.

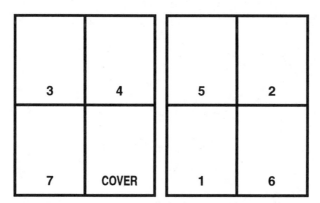

Step One:
To make your own dummy book, fold an 8-1/2"-x-11" sheet of paper into quarters and number each section "cover" and one through seven as shown.

Step Two:
Make up a story, alone or with friends. Make cartoon characters out of yourselves or people you know personally so that your comics will be more

interesting. People love to see themselves in comics, just like in home movies or on video. Leave ninjas, superheroes, and giant robots to color comics, which specialize in that sort of thing.

Step Three:
Draw the pages on "Side A" of the dummy book on a separate sheet of paper from the pages of "Side B". Draw your comics lightly in pencil, then ink the drawings with a black ink pen. Erase the pencil lines after the ink dries. Many artists skip the penciling stage and draw directly with a pen. Either way, be sure that you do the lettering first!

Don't forget to include your name, address, the date, and a copyright notice - the word "copyright" or the symbol "©" next to your name and the year - on your minicomic.

Step Four:
Take the finished pages to a copy shop and photocopy your comics onto both sides of a sheet of paper. Make sure that the person doing the job understands that this will be made into a book, so page one must be on the back of the cover, page three on the back of page two, etc. Check to make sure that they did it right before you pay for the job.

Watch your budget and don't print more than you can use... Fifty to a hundred copies should be enough for any conceivable need. You can always run off more if you need them.

(Remember to be courteous and polite when dealing with printers! Often they are busy with other jobs that make them more money and may not understand how important your minicomics are to you.)

Step Five:

Cut the printed pages in half horizontally. Save your original art! You'll need it for future print runs.

Step Six:

Put the two halves together and fold them like a book. Make sure that the pages are in the right order!

Step Seven:

Staple the pages together near the spine.
Your minicomic is now complete!

Appendix B
What's an Apa, Doc?
by Rusty Crump

Rusty Crump, former central mailer of the esteemed comics apa CAPA-Alpha, provided the following introduction to apas, frequently the training ground for tomorrow's pros. "Apa" stands for "amateur publishing association" or "amateur press alliance", but in contrast to such acronyms as "TV" and "SPCA", "apa" is spoken as a word - like "scuba" ("self-contained underwater breathing apparatus"). Who says that comics aren't educational? Now take it away, Rusty...

An apa is nearly impossible to describe in simple terms, which may be why more people don't belong to apas. But those of us who have discovered the world of apas understand their value, in terms of networking, of catharsis, of honing creative and critical skills - even in terms of pure gossip. I guess the closest that I can get to a quick descriptor of an apa is to say that it's a town meeting, in which the "town" is any group of folks interested in the same topic. That topic may be defined broadly (comics, science fiction) or narrowly (the Teen Titans, Anne McCaffrey's Pern milieu), but either way, since the town borders are something other than geographical, something other than an actual in-person gathering is necessary to provide a sense of community. That something other is a bound mailing published on a regular basis by the apa as a whole, consisting of contributions by its members in the form of "apazines" - fanzines produced exclusively (or nearly so) for the apa and collated and distributed by an elected representative known as the official editor, central mailer, or some variation thereof.

The range in frequency for publication of mailings varies with each apa, from bi-weekly to annually and sometimes with twists: National Pasttime, a baseball apa, publishes less frequently during the off-season. During 1993 and 1994, I was the central mailer of CAPA-Alpha, the world's oldest (and, in my biased opinion, finest) apa devoted to comics. "Comics" is a fairly inclusive term, encompassing animation, comic strips, comic books, and other, related media. Since CAPA-Alpha - or K-a for short - was founded in 1964, dozens of other comics apas have been born, many of them narrower in scope: Interlac (for Legion of Super-Heroes fans), Rowrbrazzle (for "furry fandom"), the Marvel Zombie Society Apa (for Marvel fans in general), and X-Apa (for... oh, just guess).

Many apas are gathering places for professionals in the industries that those apas are formed to celebrate. K-a, for example, has seen a steady stream of pros move through its pages in its thirty-year history. In the early years there were Roy Thomas, Steve Gerber, Don and Maggie Thompson, and even, briefly, Vaughn Bodé. Wendy Pini's work made a lasting impression on K-a when she was still Wendy Fletcher; Neal Pozner, Mark Evanier, and Fred Hembeck each spent several very active years in the apa. Today, the roster is graced with the names (and contributions) of Tony Isabella and Mark Verheiden, among other pros. And who knows which fans of today will become the pros of tomorrow?

Being central mailer of K-a for two years put me in much closer day-to-day contact with the entire membership than I ever could have managed otherwise - but just reading the mailings themselves led me to several observations about the ways that industry pros, non-pros and aspiring pros relate to each other in an apa. Rather than tell tales out of school, let me just pass on some of those observations:

Sometimes the professionals join the apa because of its subject matter; writing an apazine is akin to a musician playing scales to warm up, keep the chops or the embouchure, stay in tune with their instrument (which, in such a case, is the apa member's writing or drawing talent). At the same time, industry pros who maintain an apa membership don't feel compelled to create deathless prose or the finest artwork in their apa contributions. For one thing, they're not getting paid for it in any currency but the admiration of their fellow apa members (though that can be worth more than money on days when the rent's paid up). For another, the loose, funky, semi-improvisational feel of apa contributions lends itself to quick sketches, spur-of-the-moment story ideas, free-association, and other kinds of brainstorming; the editing and polishing process comes later, away from the apa.

Some pros are members of apas *despite* their involvement in the field that their apa celebrates. They may be on the roster because it's a way to keep in touch with friends also in that apa. They may have slowly graduated from amateur to industry-pro status and are staying on out of sheer inertia. Or they may have been in fandom for so long that even after making professional sales year after year, they still consider themselves fans first and pros only after a period of mental gymnastics. And for these folks, the same appeal of writing-apazines-as-playing-scales applies, even if the lure of the apa's subject matter doesn't.

Despite its subject matter or because of it, though, industry pros join an apa because they *must create*. They *have* to write, *have* to draw, *have* to make music, and would continue to do so even if they weren't getting paid one red cent. But turning in a script or piece of artwork and receiving a check is not a social event - writing an apa contribution and feeling that small thrill when the mailing shows up in the mailbox *is*. And that's why, even though pros may work with or against the fact that they have somewhat-elevated pro status in an apa, they're there primarily for the same reason everyone else is there - for the company.

In a peaceful coexistence with the industry pros are those who *want* to be industry pros. I say "peaceful" coexistence because I've never encountered someone so mercenary as to join an apa just as a means of getting work by impressing the pros present. This isn't to say that such people don't exist, but I've been in three apas, and I've never met any. Creators aspiring to the pro ranks are in apas for pretty much the same reasons as pros themselves - to try out new material for an audience that won't pull any punches (an audience, moreover, that's knowledgeable enough in the field to make any criticisms more valid than the average), and to keep up with industry news from the insiders' viewpoint presented by pros. And while it is the height of bad manners to actively court the favor of pros in an apa (the equivalent of crashing a literary cocktail party to get John Grisham's autograph), it makes good sense for aspiring pros to put their best unpublished work in an apa contribution, without leading commentary or sense of obligation on anybody's part to critique it, knowing that it will be noticed by the pros in the apa. It's done every month in hundreds of apas. But again, and I can't stress this enough, an apa is a social occasion. If what was once fun turns into another day at the office, people leave, and the apa withers and dies. An apa is not at all like the publishers' booths at big comics conventions where editors critique the work of a mile-long line of hopefuls. It's a town meeting; it's a cocktail party; it's a workshop where creators sharpen their skills - it's all of these things.

If the concept of apas intrigues you, arm yourself with a copy of *The New Moon Directory*, which is generally considered the best resource for keeping up with the hundreds of apas in existence. Editor/publisher Eric Watts updates his database continually and, in true fannish/'zinester tradition, self-publishes the revised *NMD* every year. Be warned, though, that some of the older, more established apas have a long waiting list for entry to the roster - K-a's is currently two to three years, but K-a is not necessarily the be-all and end-all of comics apas. You might join a couple of apas at once, or write for spec copies of half a dozen, to find the group where you fit in. Once you're in an apa, if you're an aspiring pro, run your best work up the flagpole and see who salutes.

And have fun!

Appendix C
Playing in the Majors
by Jerry Ordway (with the Editor)

As revealed earlier in this volume, Jerry Ordway's first professional comics assignment came fifteen years ago, when he inked a short story for DC's Mystery in Space. *A job as inker on the monthly* All-Star Squadron *followed, and two years later, when penciler Rich Buckler left the series, Jerry took over the full art chores on that series. He later branched out even further, handling both the writing and the artwork for DC's* Adventures of Superman. *Largely self-taught but a consummate professional, with experience in a variety of creative disciplines, Jerry seemed like the perfect source for further examination of what to expect when submitting material to a larger, mainstream comics publisher. I hope that you agree. The boldface type of the following interview represents the editor; Jerry speaks in normal text.*

Was your entry to DC as an inker a case of you actively seeking out inking work or of simply not being accepted as a penciler and trying an alternative?

I submitted samples that were penciled *and* inked, and I think that [the editors] needed inkers more than they needed pencilers at that time. I had a fairly clean ink line, too, so that probably helped.

It was a way to get into comics, so I certainly wasn't going to turn that down - even though I was a little disappointed. I knew that I was going to get a chance [to pencil] - or *make* a chance - later on.

Were you submitting copies of the pencils and then inked versions of the pencils?

No. I didn't even have traditional samples. I certainly wouldn't recommend showing samples like I did to get work; my samples didn't show anything of what I could do as far as storytelling or laying out a page - [they] just showed that I could draw and that I could ink.

One of the most frequent recommendations that I hear artists and editors give is "Don't just show us pin-ups. Tell a story." But it does seem that a lot of popular comic-book artists today are using pin-ups - or

at least collage - as opposed to straightforward panel-to-panel storytelling.

Right. But it's a pin-up style that applies itself to comics. You still need to be able to tell a story with it, and you need to show that you can draw a lot of different things. Superhero comics *are* figures in tights for the most part, but you still have to have those figures interacting [with more realistic settings], and that's where you need to do your homework, so to speak.

If I'm an artist who does want to show my portfolio to a Marvel or a DC, and I've been told to submit pages of actual continuity, where do I get a story? Do I just make up a short scene? Do I send in for a sample plot? Do I submit a whole full-length story that I've written myself?

If you were looking to break in as a writer, then you could submit a story of your own in various forms - the [written] plot, then maybe a couple of sample pages, each in a different stage in production. But if you're looking to "just" draw, to become a penciler, then make up a short sequence.

I always tell people that a good way of doing it is to work up a sequence of Clark Kent at *The Daily Planet* when something happens and he has turn into Superman. You could do two or three pages: A page of Clark Kent interacting with the other people at *The Planet*, showing that you can draw everday stuff - clothes, people sitting at desks and walking and so on - and then a segue to the superhero action, the beginnings of a fight, showing that you can handle action and dynamic figures. That's not really that much of a brainteaser to come up with; everybody's seen Superman get the news, in some way, that he's needed, and pull open his shirt and fly out a window.

When you look at samples at conventions, does it seem that younger artists stress the action and superhero sequences over those shots of Clark Kent interacting with other people?

Yeah. When people come up to me, they're coming up to me for my *opinion*; I'm not able to offer them a job. And I'd say that most of the time, people have [almost exclusively] action shots - which maybe is what [*How to Draw Comics the Marvel Way*] had stressed. That's important, but I think that the other stuff is equally important.

If you're able to draw a convincing action page with dynamic figures and storytelling, of course, it's likely that you'll be hired over somebody who *can't* do that - who can draw very well, but whose stuff doesn't have any *life*. The emphasis is, and still should be, on creating exciting, action-oriented pages, but I don't like to have anybody sell themselves short.

Should pencilers try their hand at inking themselves? There's a theory that says "If you want to be a penciler, why learn to ink when you could use that time becoming a better penciler?" On the other hand, you could think of that as working your way out of half of your job opportunities.

I"e worked with other people inking my stuff, and I've inked other people's stuff, and it's fun - but I've always had the desire to ink my own work. It's a good tool to have, the ability to hold a pen and create a repro-ducible style. Maybe your penciling is your strong point - and I do hear people say "You're a penciler, forget your inking" - but I would never tell anybody that. I think that the more you can do, the more options you have. And there are a lot of people out there who would love to be able to ink their own work but absolutely never had the opportunity, never had the courage, and their technical ability with a pen is so far behind their other skills that it would be an embarrassment.

It's a dangerous thing to let anybody lead you down that road of special-izing too much, because you really need to be as versatile as possible. If penciling work dries up, you've got inking to fall back on.

To take that one step further: Should artists consider developing a lettering style as well? There are very few artists currently working in mainstream comics who are lettering their own pages - and when they do, it's usually done with a computer-lettering font, the way John Byrne has developed a [font] style based on his own hand lettering - but it seems that that might be a wave of the future.

You should certainly know how, but in most cases, that's just out of the artists' hands. I wouldn't even bother drawing [dialogue and thought] balloons in [with sample pages], because at that point you don't really need to worry about it.

Frank Miller letters his own stuff; Moebius letters his own stuff; Will Eisner letters his own stuff. Certainly all of these people have styles of which the lettering was an important part. You don" *have* to be able to do everything, but, again, if you can, it's certainly a plus.

How early on is it important for someone to be using the right tools? If I'm inking, should I be learning to use a brush versus a pen, or mark-ers, etc.?

The earlier you do any of this stuff, the earlier you become comfortable with any given tool, the better. Some people swear by inking with a brush, some people love inking with a pen. I use both in different ways. I started out really learning how to ink with a brush, and became frustrated with the quality of brushes that I was able to find, so I switched to pens. But I have the technical ability to work with both, which is good.

George Pérez was one of the first people to make a big name of inking with Rapidograph pens, and I thought that his results were fine but I would *never* recommend that to somebody. Good old india ink and a flexible pen really gives the drawing a lot more life than a technical pen or a marker could. But then there are people who get away with markers very successfully - like Alex Toth, certainly, and Gil Kane; it's just not my cup of tea. Anything that gives you a technical ability - or *facility* - to put lines down on paper is something that you should be exploring early on, even if you don't do it a lot; just the idea that you *can* do it is going to be a big plus.

Given that art stores are fairly accessible and that it's even possible to buy blue-lined Bristol board at the local comics shop, does it reflect poorly on me if I show up with samples for an editor and I haven't used quote-unquote "the right materials"?

If you're showing a sample page and it's drawn on a piece of newsprint, well, you're just not going to get very good *results*, and that's going to work against you from the beginning. I can go into any art-supply store and buy Strathmore two-ply Bristol board and rule it out myself. I did that when I did *WildStar*. You can buy a pad of paper for fifteen bucks versus spending thirty bucks for really high-quality paper - but if [art] is what you're choosing as your livelihood, then it pays to use the best materials.

The same goes for inking: You're just not going to get the results that you're looking for unless you're using good-quality pens and brushes. But a carpenter isn't going to use a lousy hammer, either.

When I was sixteen years old, I got a lightbox for my birthday, and I'm still using it. Some things, when you buy 'em, you've *got* 'em. There are certain tools that you need: You buy a good set of Rapidograph pens, and you can just buy three of them in different line widths; if you keep them clean, they'll last you years and years. Brushes or pen tips, they tend to wear out a little bit faster, but *how* you do your work is as important as *what* you're doing. All of that reflects on you.

On the other hand, if I'm looking at samples, and I see somebody who's incredibly sloppy, well, as long as that work is fine for reproduction I don't care how much white-out he's got on a page. It's not judged as a piece of fine art, it's judged as a step towards creating a comic book, y'know? So the content's still the most important part, but it does pay to use the right materials.

I'll never forget visiting Scott McCloud's table at Comicfest and seeing that his pages for *Understanding Comics* had white-out and panels pasted over other panels, and thinking "He does this just like I do!"

One of my first exposures to an actual comic-book page was years ago, when I saw a Gil Kane page from some DC book. Gil had inked it himself, and there was a blob of white-out on this one figure that looked three-dimensional! But he'd drawn over it, and that page looked fine in the comic book. That was a lesson for me: It *is* for reproduction, and as long as it holds up for reproduction, it's fine. Nowadays, I don't think that I use as much white-out as I used to, but if I have to I'll still do it.

That brings up a good point, because most of us, even if we just drew comics as a hobby when we were younger, could only look at the finished product and try to approximate the creative stages ourselves, without ever seeing the original art or knowing how it was done. Do you recommend looking at or purchasing original art to get a feel for the process?

Sure. You don't have to go out and purchase a Jim Lee page that you can't afford; there's a lot of really good professional artwork out there that you can get for ten, twenty bucks a page. If I'd had access to the comics conventions that kids have now when *I* was a kid, I certainly would've bought a John Buscema page here and there. I did it a little later; I bought a couple of these things when I was eighteen, and they were very helpful.

You need all of the steps filled in before you can do anything with comics. You have to be able to draw oversize; you have to know what size the drawing area is; you have to have an understanding of Zip-a-Tone or whatever, though they don't use it as much nowadays.

As an artist, did you usually work from plots or full scripts?

Mostly plots. When I worked with Roy Thomas, it was always plot-style. I haven't really worked full-script with many people; I think that [John] Byrne had written one full-script job for me, and that was for his own sake, getting done ahead of schedule.

I tend to like [working from plots] - I think that it's a little less restrictive. [Writers] don't always have a sense of what fits on a page, and when you're working full-script, there's no changing it, really; if you've got people saying lots of stuff, you're going to be drawing small figures just to fit all the balloons in.

Given your background as an artist, do you have to resist the temptation to provide a full script and play "cinematographer" yourself when you write for other people?

After you work with somebody for a little while, you know what they can do and what they're *going* to do. I've always tried to write fairly full - it's a plot with dialogue, and I do that as a help for the artist as well as for *me*, when the pages come back. Usually, I'll get five penciled pages at a time, and more often than not I'm expected to turn those five pages in, dialogued, at the end of the day so that they can be sent off to the letterer [*Laughs*], so you really have to know what you were thinking when you [wrote that scene] in the plot. It still allows the artist to be flexible in terms of moving stuff around, and gives them a sense of the emotions in a scene - which *I* always appreciated when I worked plot-style. It's nice to know if a character is supposed to be mad or sad or crazy or whatever, and a lot of times you don't get that direction; you see dialogue that doesn't quite match the facial expression that you drew and a little note for the inker to turn a smile into a grimace or whatever.

My experience in working with other [writers] has certainly filtered down into how I work with artists now. My plots tend to be somewhat wordy, but again, it's mostly possible dialogue; I try to paint the picture for the artist, but everybody sees the set differently. It's like reading a bestselling book and imagining who's gonna play the lead in the movie.

When one sends away for the submission guidelines at DC, the intructions for writers say to keep a proposal to one page, typed, double-spaced. And to present a story that has a beginning and middle and end, plus a hook that's going to snag the editor and make him want to see more, all in one typed, double-spaced page - it seems like an art form unto itself.

[*Laughs*] It's a good talent to have. I'm working on a regular monthly title and I still have in the back of my head that,even though it's a continuing title, each [issue's] story should have some resolution to it. It's good to have people think in very brief terms like that. That's probably *not* how they would be expected to write if they got a job - certainly, a regular plot by someone, once they were hired from that submission, would run much more than one page. But I think that [the editors] want the good idea up front; they don't want to muddle through a lot of explanation. And it's harder than a lot of people make it out to be - it's easy to type until you get tired, but it actually takes some mindwork to keep track of where the story's going at different stages.

With your track record, you're in a position to pitch a full-blown series like *The Power of Shazam.* **Does an unknown writer, or a writer/artist team, have any shot at pitching revivals of unused characters with real potential as opposed to a ten-page** *Showcase* **story with a supporting character from** *The Outsiders?*

I think that they do. But I think that a ten-page *Showcase* story is a tremendous starting point, and what usually happens then is that someone will develop some sort of relationship with a given editor. That happens with the submisson process, when you're artist *or* a writer: In a best-case scenario, you'll be submitting work to the same person over a period of time, which makes it easier for that person to see your progress, if you *are* progressing.

As an example, Mike Carlin had given work to Dan Vado - he did a *STAR Labs* mini-series for Mike. And Mike had been working with Dan for a little while, back and forth, and what came out of that was one of the Superman annuals from the *Eclipso* year, then the *STAR Labs* thing; and that experience with Mike was a proving ground for Dan to then work on *Justice League.* And I think that that's how it works; I keep reading on Compu-Serve complaints about the buddy network, where assignments are handed out to cronies and pals...

If you're not part of the loop, it may seem unfair that so much is going on *in* **the loop, but once you break in, it's probably very reassuring.**

Right. And what most people should be working towards is breaking into the loop. There's a lot to be said for just getting your foot in the door. One of the negative aspects that catches up with people is that most of us work on one project a month, and you tend to work with the same people. In my case, I've worked a lot with Mike Carlin, and I *like* Mike, we get along very well, and we know what to expect from each other. But if something happened and Mike left DC, or got out of comics or whatever, that would put *me* at a disadvantage because I don't have a rapport with other people. So the downside is there to the fact that it is more rewarding to work with people whom you know and like and respect.

Send submissions to different editors, but try to get a sense of having them know *you.* Take the criticism for what it's worth, and try to improve the next batch, or tailor it towards whatever a given editor is looking for, and just get into the loop somehow. In the writer's case it's a little harder, because art is something that you can "read" quickly, whereas writing is something that's a little harder to get across.

I hear it said that there's always an opening for a new artist, because so many artists are already overworked, but if there's a writing position to be filled the chances are good that there's a writer out there who's already in the loop with time in his schedule to write it.

I think that [drawing] is more labor-intensive than [writing], but I don't think that I'd *ever* be comfortable writing two projects at once. I guess some people have the ability to map out separate backstories and everything else, but I've always been an all-my-eggs-in-one-basket kind of guy. I couldn't envision doing something like that, trying to juggle a couple of books, but I think that Mark Waid is a good example of that - Waid is suddenly writing *everything*, and so far, it's all at a very high level. But there's a point, I think, at which a lot of guys will burn out.

DC's rate structure for years favored the writers, and still does, royalty-wise. That [structure] was instituted by [then-executive editor] Dick Giordano - an artist - who told me many times that by favoring the writers he was hoping to give writers a bit of an equal footing with the artists so that they *wouldn't* have to write five books a month to make a living. And the way that the rates are set up, if you write one book a month you're really in the same boat as someone who *inks* one book a month; you can certainly make a living doing one or two books.

I'd imagine that the rate structure varies greatly, especially if you're up in the fan-favorite stratosphere. At what point can you expect to support yourself full-time as a writer, or a penciler, or an inker?

The rates do vary greatly from person to person and from book to book; I think that the Superman books are pretty much a lock on the top rate [at DC]. The top rate for writing as *I* know it is a hundred bucks a page. It isn't like you're living in a mansion, but it's a pretty good salary. If you get a royalty, of course, that's extra, though not much is *earning* royalities these days.

For a penciler to be drawing a book - it's a lot of work to be drawing a twenty-two-page book month in and month out, but the financial rewards just through your page rate if you're getting a good rate, or top rate, are pretty decent. It's been awhile since I've drawn anything [regularly], but it's gotta be up around two hundred bucks a page. With *Superman*, I was getting top rate after a couple of years; someone else can get more by virtue of having a contract that offers them a bonus for every issue, but based purely on rate structure that would be the top rate. It's still decent enough money if you can get the work.

To wrap up: Do you often notice anything that aspiring writers and artists don't think of when trying to break in?

I'd certainly stress that if you're submitting work to DC, try drawing DC characters. What you're doing when you're submitting work, especially if you're doing it in person, is submitting *yourself*, really. I have friends who are really good artists who just have *horrible* attitudes, and attitude is such a big part of any job - *any* job. If you're in an office situation, you can have someone who just doesn't get along with anybody, who's not gonna get promoted, whereas you could have somebody who's not as hard a worker or not as *good* a worker but who's genuinely pleasant to work with who *will* be promoted.

In any given situation, an editor is going to want to work with somebody who's pleasant and somebody who's nice to deal with. If you're a pain in the ass, you're not gonna have that advantage; you could be the best artist in the world, but if you're a jerk about it it's not gonna do that much for you. I've known people coming up through comics, when I was coming up, people out there - it's fine to have ego about you, but it shouldn't overwhelm your work. Any creative person needs an ego, but you have to understand that you're not gonna draw the top book for the company right away, and you're not going to get anywhere by talking down whoever's doing the stuff for a certain editor - "I can do that better that so-and-so." That just puts you that much further in the hole.

I'll give you an example of something like that that happened recently: A guy wrote a letter to *Power of Shazam* saying how he had all these great ideas that would make *Shazam* this big success, and he really didn't understand that he was stepping over the line. You obviously want to build yourself up as the guy for the job, but the problem is that when you send a letter like that to an editor, the editor's already *chosen* someone for the job. Never try to build yourself up at the expense of somebody else. A lot of people just don't understand that. Whoever you are, you should be trying to do the best work *you* can do.

Resources

This isn't exactly a bibliography or a list of recommended reading, because it covers more than just books. It's a guide to what the title up above says - resources. Hopefully, whatever aspect of the comics community appealed to you most in the pages preceeding, you'll find an avenue for further exploration here.

Remember, though, that the best resource remains the community itself, made up of interrelating networks of dedicated, talented, often crazy but usually loveable people who aren't entirely unlike yourself and who will, nine times out of ten, gladly give to you of their time. Search out some friends, mentors, and collaborators, and, above all, have fun.

Publishers

The following publishers are active within the comics industry, and offer a broad spectrum of form and content in their product. Some publish nothing but creator-owned material, and in those cases a completed project - or at least a very fully realized proposal - is preferable for submission. Others only publish material incorporating characters and concepts owned by the publishing company itself, in which case a very succinct story pitch or a handful of pages of artwork is the best choice. Still others go both ways and a few ways in-between.

Editorial needs - and editors themselves - come and go. When contacting a publisher, ProMotion *recommends addressing a brief, polite letter clearly marked "Attn: Submissions Editor", accompanied by a standard-sized SASE (self-addressed, stamped envelope), as a first step in seeking information on submission guidelines. Remember that an editor's priority is getting his or her current projects out the door, however, so a response may not be as personal or immediate as you'd like. Sending a blind submission is not a good idea, and virtually guarantees you a delayed response - if any response at all.*

Sometimes, publishers need office help as much as they do creative talent. If you live near one of the addresses listed below, or are willing to relocate for a school internship, summer job, or even post-collegiate entry-level position, consider contacting an editor about an internship. While ProMotion *focuses on the storytelling aspect of the comics industry, there are many facets to the publishing business, and it can be a valuable experience to learn a bit of everything.*

Please note that ProMotion *does not guarantee that any of the publishers below will respond to your inquiries to your satisfaction, nor that all of them necessarily accept even the most splendid of submissions. It just doesn't hurt to ask.*

Acclaim Comics houses three imprints: Valiant, home to such superhero and action/adventure series as *Magnus: Robot Fighter* and *Solar: Man of the*

Atom; Armada, whose comic books are based on such popular properties as the collectible card game *Magic: The Gathering*; and Windjammer, an imprint expressly for creator-owned properties. You can reach Acclaim at **275 Seventh Ave., New York, NY 10001.**

Aeon Press is the publisher of such fine creator-owned projects as *The Desert Peach*, written and illustrated by *ProMotion* contributor Donna Barr. Write to Aeon at **5014-D Roosevelt Way NE, Seattle, Wash. 98105.**

Antarctic Press has published a variety of creator-owned series, from founder Ben Dunn's *Ninja High School* to *ProMotion* contributor Terry Moore's original run of *Strangers in Paradise*. Contact Antarctic at **7272 Wurzbach #204, San Antonia, Tex. 78240.**

Archie Comics is one of the oldest and most successful publishers in the comics industry. Its core series, featuring the Archie gang in such books as *Archie, Jughead, Betty and Veronica*, and *Archie's Pals and Gals*, draw upon such talent as comics veterans Dan DeCarlo and *ProMotion* contributor Stan Goldberg. Archie also publishes *The Flintstones*, *The Jetsons*, and other titles based on the Hanna-Barbera cartoon stable, as well as such licensed properties as *Sonic the Hedgehog* and *Teenage Mutant Ninja Turtles*. Write to Archie at **325 Fayette Ave., Mamaroneck, NY 10543-2318.**

Bongo Comics is the place to find comics based on Matt Groening's *The Simpsons*, including such spinoffs as *Krusty the Clown* and *Radioactive Man*. Bongo inaugurated a creator-owned imprint, Zongo, last summer. Contact Bongo at **1999 Ave. of the Stars, Los Angeles, Calif. 90067.**

Caliber Press publishes a very diverse array of comics material, including such creator-owned properties as David Mack's *Kabuki* and Bernie Mireault's *The Jam* and the acclaimed anthology *Negative Burn*. *ProMotion* contributor Matt Feazell's minicomics work was collected by Caliber last July in the trade paperback *Ert!* You can reach Caliber at **11904 Farmington Rd., Livonia, Mich. 48150.**

Chaos! Comics is best known for the *Evil Ernie* series and its spinoff, *Lady Death*, created by publisher Brian Pulido and brought to life by artists like Steven Hughes. You can reach Chaos! at **7349 Via Paseo Del Sur, Suite 515-208, Scottsdale, Ariz. 85258.**

Claypool Comics publishes such supernatural situation comedies as *Soulsearchers and Company*, co-created and written by *ProMotion* contributor

Peter David. *PM* contributor Neil Vokes has illustrated stories for both *Soulsearchers* and Claypool's *Elvira, Mistress of the Dark*. Write to Claypool at **647 Grand Ave., Leonia, NJ 07605**.

Dark Horse Comics publishes nearly every kind of comics under the sun, licensing such properties as *Star Wars, Aliens,* and *The Shadow*; publishing a company-owned line of superhero titles that includes *The Mask* and *Barb Wire*; and showcasing new and veteran "alternative" creators in *Dark Horse Presents*. Dark Horse is also home to the Legend imprint, whose founders include Frank Miller, Mike Mignola, Dave Gibbons, and *ProMotion* contributor John Byrne. Contact Dark Horse at **10956 SE Main St., Milwaukie, Ore. 97222**.

DC Comics is the oldest publisher of comic books in existence, and the second largest operating today. Its DC Universe line includes such seminal superhero series as *Superman, Batman, Wonder Woman, The Flash,* and *The Power of Shazam* - the latter two written by *ProMotion* contributors Mark Waid and Jerry Ordway - while its Vertigo imprint covers such acclaimed projects as *The Sandman, Hellblazer,* and *Swamp Thing*. DC also publishes the legendary magazine *Mad* and, through both Vertigo and Paradox Press, such innovative work as *ProMotion* contributor Howard Cruse's acclaimed *Stuck Rubber Baby*. DC can be reached at **1700 Broadway Ave., New York, NY 10019**.

Drawn and Quarterly Publications is best known for its eponymous anthology and creator-owned projects like Joe Matt's *Peepshow*, Chester Brown's *Underwater,* and *PM* contributor Mary Fleener's *Slutburger*. Write to D&Q at **5550 Jeanne Mance St. #16, Montreal PQ H2V 4K6**.

Gladstone Comics publishes new and reprint material from the likes of Carl Barks and Don Rosa, based on the rich stable of old-time Walt Disney characters in such series as *Donald Duck* and *Uncle Scrooge Adventures*. Gladstone can be reached at **PO Box 2079, Prescott, Ariz., 86302**.

Fantagraphics Books is home to Peter Bagge's *Hate* and Jaime and Gilbert Hernandez' *Love and Rockets,* as well as *The Comics Journal* and such high-quality reprint series as *The Complete Crumb Comics*. Write to Fantagraphics at **7563 Lake City Way NE, Seattle, Wash. 98115**.

Harris Comics resurrected Warren Publishing's *Vampirella*, now written by *ProMotion* contributor Tom Sniegoski. Other Harris titles include *Rook* and *Hyde-25*. Write to Harris at **1115 Broadway Ave., New York, NY 10010**.

Image Comics took the comics industry by storm when its founding members walked away from their freelance assignments at Marvel Comics and announced their intention to publish their own creations. Image's top series include *Spawn*, from Todd McFarlane Productions; *Youngblood*, from Rob Liefeld's Extreme Studios; Jim Valentino's *ShadowHawk*, also at Extreme; *The Savage Dragon*, from Erik Larsen's Highbrow Entertainment; Jim Lee's *WildCATs* and *StormWatch*, from WildStorm Productions; and *CyberForce*, from Marc Silvestri's Ballistic Studios. Other Image publications, also creator-owned, include *ProMotion* contributor Kurt Busiek's *Astro City* and Jeff Smith's small-press phenomenon *Bone*. Image's central address is **PO Box 25468, Ahaheim, Calif. 92825**; write there for directions on contacting each studio.

Kitchen Sink Press lives up to its name, publishing everything but. It's home to *ProMotion* contributor Jeff Nicholson's new series, *Father and Son*; new and old work from comics master Will Eisner; and archival material featuring the work of Alex Toth, Robert Crumb, and others. You can reach Kitchen Sink at **320 Riverside Dr., Northampton, Mass. 01060**.

Malibu Comics has a diverse publishing history, recently retrenching its position in the marketplace as a sister company to Marvel Comics and relaunching such superhero titles as *Prime*, *Mantra*, and *UltraForce*. Write to Malibu Comics at **26707 Agoura Rd., Calabasas, Calif. 91302**.

Marvel Comics is the largest comic-book publisher in North America, and has funneled its Marvel Universe characters - most co-created by living legend (and, yes, *ProMotion* contributor) Stan Lee - into television and toy-store successes as well. Its core titles include superhero series like *Captain America*, *The Incredible Hulk*, *The Amazing Spider-Man*, and *The Uncanny X-Men*, but licensed properties from *Barbie* to *Beavis and Butt-Head* to *Beauty and the Beast* are also published under the Marvel banner. Write to Marvel at **397 Park Ave. South, New York, NY 10016**.

Milestone Media has dedicated its comic books to a blend of superhero soap opera that incorporates characters and creators from various ethnic and ideological mixes, as seen in such acclaimed series as *Icon* and *Static*, published through arrangement with DC Comics. Milestone can be reached at **Suite 409, 119 West 23rd St., New York, NY 10011**.

Slave Labor Graphics is home to *ProMotion* contributor Scott Saavedra's *Java Town* and a host of other idiosyncratic projects that display the full potential of creator-owned small-press work - such as *Milk and Cheese* and

Hectic Planet, from Evan Dorkin, and *Action Girl Comics*, edited and designed by *PM* contributor Sarah Dyer. Contact Slave at **979 South Bascom Ave., San José, Calif. 95128.**

Topps Comics publishes almost exclusively licensed material, though from a variety of sources, including *Zorro*, *The X-Files*, and *Duckman*. Topps can be reached at **1 Whitehall St., New York, NY 10004.**

Warp Graphics began life as the imprint under which Wendy and Richard Pini self-published their comic book *Elfquest*, but it has grown into a cottage industry in which the Pinis contribute to and oversee the production of a variety of titles based on their characters and concepts. Working with them are such talented writers and artists as *ProMotion* contributors Barry Blair and Gary Kato. Write to Warp at **43 Haight Ave., Poughkeepsie, NY 12603.**

Self-Publishers

Self-publishers are a very special subsection of publishers who - that's right - publish their own (and, usually, only their own) work. With half-a-handful of exceptions, the following list is limited to those self-publishers who are represented with entries in ProMotion; *a comprehensive survey of all self-publishers in and around comics is another project entirely.*
These publishers are listed here for essentially two reasons: (1) Their comics may not be represented in your local comic-book store - if you're lucky enough to have such a thing - but, after reading the entries in this book, you may find that you want to check out the work of a contributor whose perspective you really enjoyed. Feel free to write to them with an inquiry about purchasing some of their comic books. (2) Working creatively in comics can be a lonely and scary job; self-publishing, even lonelier and scarier. It's likely that the folks below know where you've been and where you want to go, and most of them will be only too happy to answer questions for you. While you're writing, of course, feel free to send an inquiry about purchasing some of their comic books...

Aardvark-Vanaheim is the "corporate" identity of self-publishing guru Dave Sim, creator of *Cerebus*. Recently, *Cerebus* has devoted nearly as much space to Dave's views on the changing tides in comics' direct market (the publisher-distributor-retailer chain in which comics specialty shops participate) - and, specifically, on what it means to the self-publisher - as it has to his fiction. You can reach Dave at **PO Box 1674, Station C, Kitchener, Ontario N2G 4R2.**

Adhesive Comics is a publishing collective co-founded by Shannon Wheeler, through which he publishes *Too Much Coffee Man*. Inquiries about getting enough coffee can be sent to **PO Box 5372, Austin, Tex. 78763-5372.**

All sorts of **Action Girl Comics** can be had from Sarah Dyer, a *ProMotion* contributor who self-publishes a bunch of 'zines on a variety of subjects, including - but not limited to - comics. Write to Sarah at **PO Box 060380, Staten Island, NY 10306.**

Blazer Unlimited is home to *PM* contributor Daniel Reed's latest effort, *Retro-Dead*, which at this writing was scheduled to kick off in October. It Reed's acclaimed science-fiction epic, *New World Order*. Send correspondence and orders to **101 West 12th St., New York, NY 10011-8108.**

Boardwalk Press brought you this very book. If you're interested in checking out the minicomics work of *ProMotion* author/editor Brian Saner-Lamken, including *Falling*, an honest-to-gosh "24-hour comic", write to **PO Box 362, Wynnewood, Penna. 19096-0362.** This is the also the address from which you can order additional copies of *ProMotion*; see the copyright page for further details.

Cartoonists across America isn't quite a self-publishing operation, but it is spearheaded by *PM* contributor Phil Yeh, creator of such CAA releases as *Patrick Rabbit*, *The Winged Tiger*, and *Voyage to Veggie Isle*. Check out some of this fine work by writing to **PO Box 670, Lompoc, Calif. 93438-0670.**

CLG Comics is the one-man publishing house of *PM* contributor Bruce Chrislip, whose *Paper Tales* cleans out the dark, recessed corners of his brain. Drop him a line at **8057 13th St. NW, Seattle, Wash. 98117.**

ProMotion contributor Stan Lynde offers reprint collections of his comic strips, new graphic novels, and *Rick O'Shay, Hipshot, and Me*, a book of memoirs, from his **Cottonwood Publishing.** You can reach Stan at **2340 Trumble Creek Rd., Kalispell, Mont. 59901-6713.**

Exhibit 'A' Press is *PM* **contributor** Batton Lash's imprint for his comic book *Wolff and Byrd, Counselors of the Macabre* - it's scary, but it's legal. The address is **4657 Cajon Way, San Diego, Calif. 92115.**

Explorer Press is the publishing imprint formed by *ProMotion* contributor Terry Collins and his collaborator, Bill Neville, for their new series, *Explorers*. They can be reached at **PO Box 1907, Mount Airy, NC 27030.**

Fiasco Comics is home to *ProMotion* contributor Don Simpson's *Bizarre Heroes*, the satirical self-published superhero smash of the century - give or take a hundred years. Last spring, Fiasco released its first trade-paperback compilation, *Bizarre Heroes: The Apocalypse Affiliation*. Don would love to hear from you at **PO Box 44326, Pittsburgh, Penna. 15205.**

King Hell Press devotes its energies these days to creator/writer/artist/letterer/publisher Rick Veitch's comics dream diary, *Rare Bit Fiends*, a fantastic exercise in which readers can share: Rick publishes other folks' dreams, in both text and comics form, in each issue. Write to Roarin' Rick at **PO Box 1371, West Townshend, Vt. 05379.**

Nice Day Comix publishes handmade comics of the same name - and others - as crafted by the fevered brain of *ProMotion* contributor Randy H. Crawford and a bevy of collaborators. Pass along some of your own creations to **911 Park St. SW, Grand Rapids, Mich. 49504-6241**, and he'll likely respond in kind.

Matt Feazell has built an unassuming minicomics empire under the banner of **Not Available Comics**, which actually does have quite a few publications available, including the graphic-novel-in-progress *The Death of Antisocialman*, which you can check out by sending some coins to **3367 Bristow, Detroit, Mich. 48212.**

Pen and Ink Comics publishes *Wandering Star*, the acclaimed series wrought by Teri S. Wood, a swell person even though she's *not* a *ProMotion* contributor. You can reach Teri at **Box 817, Banning, Calif. 92220.**

Rubber Blanket Press is responsible for the outstanding, if erratic, *Rubber Blanket*, a comics anthology showcasing the work of publishers David Mazzucchelli, Richmond Lewis, and others. Check it out by contacting them at **PO Box 3067, Uptown Station, Hoboken, NJ 07030.**

Screaming Dodo Studios is the bouncing baby bird of *ProMotion* contributor Brian Clopper, through which he plans to self-publish *Fever Pitch*, resurrecting characters from his *Partners in Pan DEMONium*. Write to Brian at **21 Valley Park Ct., Damascus, Md. 20872.**

SpareTime Studios consists of a swell bunch of guys whose *ProMotion* appearance was disrupted by a series of technological snafus. They publish *Primitives*, a comic book created with equal parts talent and heart. Drop them a line at **PO Box 45432, Seattle, Wash. 98145.**

The 3D Zone is the dimension of comics space occupied by *ProMotion* contributor Ray Zone, publisher of fine 3D comic books and other archival material. You haven't seen 3D until you've seen this stuff. Access the zone via **1945 Hillhurst Ave. #4, Los Angeles, Calif. 90027**.

Further Study

You might think that, armed with this copy of ProMotion *for inspiration, you're ready to embark on a career in comics. And maybe you are. But I wouldn't be doing my job if I didn't remind you that there are other resources worth checking out, no matter what area of the comics world you feel is your home.*
While there's no substitute for Just Doing It - getting your hands dirty with some pencil and paper and bringing what's inside you out into the world - education, advice, and encouragement are available from such people and places if you want them. So we're heading out with this list of suggestions for further experiences, in books, online, and elsewhere. Tell 'em ProMotion *sent ya!*

America Online - AOL for short - is one of the two largest online services in operation. You need a computer and a modem to connect to AOL, but once you're hooked up you'll meet a whole new set of friends. DC Comics (Keyword: DC) and the industry magazine *Wizard: The Guide to Comics* (Keyword: Wizard) both have their own sections, where you can chat in real time with other comics fans and, often, pros as well, from all over the country and beyond. The *Star Trek*/Comics/TV/*Star Wars* message boards in the Science Fiction section (Keyword: Science Fiction) are host to many non-DC readers, and regular chat sessions are scheduled there as well. Call **1-800-203-1600** for a startup kit.

You can get ahold of a good likeness of what professional comics artist generally use from **Blue Line Pro**. As Jerry Ordway noted a few short pages ago, you *can* work on just about anything at just about any size, but your inexperience will be obvious to editors and collaborators. The vast majority of artists use industry-standard 11x17" Bristol board, one-and-a-half times the size of the eventual printed page. BLP offers a variety of page types - many of which are available in a sample set, *Create Your Own Comic Book*, which also includes a character template, layout pages, a cover page, and an instructional comic book - but you really don't need to pay for "layout pages". The company's clean, white, standard blue-lined finishing pages, though, are just what the doctor ordered when it comes to the real thing. If you can't find a set at a nearby comics shop, write to the company at **264 Main St., Florence, Ky. 41042** or call **1-800-425-8546**.

Legendary comics auteur Will Eisner literally wrote the book on the comics form - *Comics and Sequential Art*, virtually the *only* book on the subject until *Understanding Comics* came along a half-dozen years later. Generously seasoned with examples from Eisner's own work, *Comics and Sequential Art* explores such areas as imagery, timing, the frame, and the melding of words and art into a cohesive unit. If you're a serious student of the comics medium, your bookshelf is incomplete without it. *C&SA* was scheduled for another printing as *ProMotion* was going to press; try to find copies through a friend or a well-stocked comics shop, or contact the publisher, Poorhouse Press, at **8333 West McNab Rd., Suite 114, Tamarac, Fla. 33321**. Also, most libraries and general-interest booksellers will trace a book for order using its ISBN [International Standard Book Number]; *C&SA*'s is **0-9614728-0-2** in paperback and **0-9614728-0-4** in hardcover.

Comics Buyer's Guide is the only weekly journal serving all corners of the comics industry - fans, retailers, creators, and publishers alike. Aspiring writers and artists should pay particular attention to the classified ads, wherein editors, publishers, and fellow creators often put out a call for help. It's also a good and inexpensive place to advertise, if you're planning to self-publish comics of any kind, and its retailer directory becomes an instant mailing list for potential customers if you want to place product directly in stores. Other useful sections include a listing of coming creator appearances, and review and opinions columns from the likes of *ProMotion* contributors Tony Isabella, Bob Ingersoll, and Peter David. To request subscription information or a sample copy, write to *CBG* at **700 East State St., Iola, Wis. 54990** with "Attn: Subscription Info" or "Attn: Sample Copy Request", as appropriate, clearly marked on the envelope.

Comics Pro Magazine began publication just months before *ProMotion* went to press, but based on its early offerings it's a must-have for nearly anyone in *ProMotion*'s audience. A number of professional writers and artists share their tips monthly on everything from how to prepare a script to how to prepare for self-employment taxes. For a copy of the most recent issue, send $4 to West Wind Publishing at at **252 Robinson Dr., Morris, Ill. 60450**; subscription rates can be found in the ad at the back of this book.

CompuServe's Comics and Animation Forum is, in many ways, the flip side of the chat rooms on America Online. Whereas AOL is heavier on real-time conversation, the bulk of the give-and-take on CompuServe comes from the message threads, which Forum members read and respond to at their leisure. There *are* conference rooms in the Forum, however, and scheduled events include a Breaking In conference run once a month by artist Rob Davis. For more information on joining the Forum (and CompuServe itself), E-mail sysop Doug Pratt at **dpratt@compuserve.com**.

Dynamic Drawing is a series of books for the student of figure drawing authored by Burne Hogarth, an acclaimed artist and cartoonist and a co-founder of New York's School of Visual Arts. The hardcover volumes include *Dynamic Figure Drawing, Drawing the Human Head, Drawing Dynamic Hands, Dynamic Anatomy, Dynamic Light and Shade,* and *Dynamic Wrinkles and Drapery,* and are available in many mass-market bookstores. There are many other fine art books on the human form, of course, and figure drawing is by *no* means the only necessary component of successful comics art, but Hogarth's books are a good place to start. If you find them in you local bookshop, art-supply store, or library, take it from there. The publisher, Watson-Guptill Publications, can be reached at **1515 Broadway Ave., New York, NY 10036**.

Factsheet Five is the self-proclaimed "Definitive Guide to the 'Zine Revolution". It is published quarterly and reviews a staggering number of 'zines that involve an even more staggering variety of topics - including comics. To order a sample copy and find out how to submit your own minicomics and/or 'zines for review, send $6 to **PO Box 170099, San Francisco, Calif. 94117**, in a check payable to *Factsheet Five*.

Lurene Haines, herself a distinguished comics creator, provides comprehensive inside advice on just what the title says in ***Getting into the Business of Comics***. Chapter by chapter and step by step, Haines drives home the importance of being professional, and includes valuable information on contracts, legal practices, and agenting. *Getting into the Business of Comics* should be on your shelves right next to *ProMotion*, and if you can't find a copy in your neck of the woods, write to Stabur Press at **11904 Farmington Rd., Livonia, Mich. 48150**.

British writer/editor/cartoonist Alan McKenzie produced ***How to Draw and Sell Comics Strips for Newspapers and Comic Books*** some years back, providing a very detailed walk-through of the methodologies of comics creation covered in *ProMotion*'s preface, with copious illustrations. While there remains no substitute for hands-on experience and personal attention from working pros, *How to Draw and Sell...* is an excellent source for artists looking to study specific tools and techniques. It was released in the US in hardcover with an ISBN of **0-89134-214-1** by F&W Publications, **1507 Dana Ave., Cincinnati, Oh. 45207**.

The New Moon Directory, recommended by Rusty Crump in his appendix on apas, is a definite must-have for anyone interested in further research on the topic. You can order a copy directly from editor/publisher Eric Watts at **346 Carpenter Dr., Atlanta, Ga. 30328-5030**. Specific apas that may be of interest and their contact people at time of publication, from whom you can recommend a recent mailing to see if the apa is for you, include:

APA-APA (the Aspiring Professionals Association apa), available from Stan Koczkodaj at **1051 Taylor Dr., Folcroft, Pa. 19032**.

APA-5 (a general-interest apa through which many of today's pros got their start), available from Robin Ator at **9939 North Syracuse, Portland, Ore. 97203**.

CAPA-Alpha (the longest-running comics apa in existence, with which no less than five *ProMotion* contributors are affiliated), available from Hurricane Heeran at **PO Box 18617, Encino, Calif. 91416**.

'Nuff Said (an apa about comics and just about everything else under the sun), available from Gregory Hecht at **32-02 Fox Run Dr., Plainsboro, NJ 08536**.

Shoptalk (an apa for comics professionals and aspiring pros), available from Steve Addlesee at **852 East 8475 South, Sandy, Ut. 94094**.

The School of Visual Arts, mentioned in this book on more than one occasion, offers a good environment for the serious aspiring comics artist. For application information, write to the admissions office at **209 East 23rd St., New York, NY 10010** or call **1-212-592-2100**.

SVA isn't the *only* comics-art college around, but it is one of the few. The legendary **Joe Kubert School of Cartoon and Graphic Art** has turned out some major talents in the field, and can be reached at **37 Myrtle Ave., Dover, NJ 07801**. And **The Savannah College of Art and Design** has a growing sequential-art program; for more information, write to the admissions office at **342 Bull St., PO Box 3146, Savannah, Ga. 31402-3146**.

If you go the minicomics route, *PM* contributor Matt Feazell suggests that you join **The Small Press Network** by sending copies of your work to Feazell himself at **3867 Bristow, Detroit, Mich., 48212**; to Ian Shires at *Self-Publisher*, **5621 Flowerdale Ave. #31, Cleveland, Oh 44144-4109**; to Max Traffic at *The White Buffalo Gazette*, **PO Box 2453, Butler, Pa. 16003**; and to Ronald Thomas-Fleming at *Lead Balloons*, **PO Box 1528, Ypsilanti, Mich. 48197**. Each of these folks will help spread the word about your creations.

In *Understanding Comics*, Scott McCloud has explored the "language" of comics using the medium itself - the book is presented in comics form, and is a great read for entertainment value alone. To the student of comics, however, it's an invaluable educational tool as well. If you can't find it in your local bookstore or comics shop, write to Kitchen Sink Press at **320 Riverside Dr., Northampton, Mass. 01060**, for a catalog and ordering information; the ISBN is **0-87816-243-7**. You will read this book again and again, and have fun doing it.

Last but not least: *Wizard: The Guide to Comics* has included a fair number of articles on writing and drawing for comics among its splashy, irreverent, and immensely popular pages. Its editorial focus has also widened beyond the usually cover-featured hot superhero stuff, and if you look past the occasional juvenile humor, it's not a bad magazine at all. If you're a regular comic-book reader, you probably know what *Wizard* is, but in case you don't, it's available on m any mass-market magazine racks these days. To subscribe directly from Wizard Press, write to the mag at **151 Wells Ave., Congers, NY 10920-2064** with "Attn: Subscription Info" clearly marked on the envelope.

Index

The following index covers creators, characters, companies, comic-book series, and select other items mentioned in the preceeding pages. Pages marked in boldface feature entries about - or, in applicable cases, written by - the indexed person or property; an underlined page denotes the indexee as the subject of or contributor to an illustration on that page. People's proper names are indexed by surname (look for Byrne, John, not John Byrne) with the exception of names used in titles of publications (look for Dick Tracy, not Tracy, Dick).

Aardvark-Vanaheim 37, 130, **169**
Abraham Lincoln, The New Adventures of 13
Abstract Studio 102
Acclaim Comics **165** [see also Valiant]
Action Comics 36, 98, 138
Action Girl Comics 56-57, 169-170
Adams, Douglas 135
Adams, Neal 104, 141
Adhesive Comics 139, **170**
Adkins, Dan 54
Adventures of Superman, The [see *Superman*]
Adventures of the Mask, The [see *Mask*]
Aeon Press 19-20, **166**
Airboy 96
Aircel Comics 22
Akin, Ian 115
Aladdin 66
Alf 124
Aliens 167
Aliens: Labyrinth 140
All-Star Squadron 108-109, 156
Alley Oop 54
Allred, Michael 92
Alpha Flight 117
Alpha Productions 27
Amazing Cynicalman, The [see *Cynicalman*]

Amazing Heroes 48, 61, 92, 119, 137
Amazing High Adventures 85
Amazing Spider-Man, The [see *Spider-Man*]
Ambush Bug 138
America Online **172**-173
Americomics 115
Anarchy Comics 63
Anderson, Brent 33
AnnRuel Studios 16
Antarctic Press 66, 102, **166**
Antisocialman, The Death of 62, 171
APA-APA **175**
APA-5 **175**
Apple Comics 76, 134-135
Aquaman 53, 88
Aragonés, Sergio 144
Archibald, Joe 129
Archie 1, 74, 77
Archie 58, 141, 166
Archie, Little 69
Archie Comics 44, 73-75, 83, 93, 132, 137, **166**
Archie Meets the Punisher 73, 93
Archie's Pals and Gals 166
Argus 78
Armstrong, Robert 65
Asterix 141
Astro City, Kurt Busiek's 31, 33, 168
Atlantis Chronicles, The 53
Atom, The 129

Augustyn, Brian 84
Auster, Paul 101
Avengers, The 95, 115
Axis Comics 112
Ayers, Dick **16-17**

Babe 36
Badger 78
Bagge, Peter 132, 167
Ballistic Studios 168
Bannon, Mike **18**
Barb Wire 54, 167
Barbie 168
Barbie Fashion 76
Barefootz 49-50
Barks, Carl 68
Baron, Mike 111-113
Barr, Donna **19-21**, 166
Batgirl 88-89
Batman 1, 23, 32, 43, 52, 83, 93, 98,
    101-102, 118, 119
Batman (comic book) 46, 87, 119,
    137, 141-142, 167; (TV series) 23, 61,
    101, 122
Batman: Digital Justice 104
Batman: The Dark Knight 27
Batman: Year One 101
Battle for a 3D World 145
Beatty, Terry 86-87
Beauty and the Beast 168
Beavis and Butt-Head 168
Beck, CC 117
Berger, Karen 102
Big Book of Death, The 93
Big Book of Urban Legends, The 42, 93
Big Book of Weirdos, The 93
Bill and Ted's Excellent Comic Book
    124
Binky's Buddies 74
Bissette, Steve 127-128
Bizarre Heroes 122-123, 171
Black Lightning 81

Blair, Barry **22**, 169
Blazer Unlimited 117, **170**
Blitz, Stefan **23**
Blood of Dracula 135
Blood Syndicate, The 69
Bloodthirst 27
Blue Line Pro **172**
Boardwalk Press 146, **170**
Bodé, Vaughn 154
Bollinger, Bruce **24-26**
Boltinoff, Murray 81
Bone 40, 103, 168
Bongo Comics **166**
Bonus Books 116
Booster Gold 88
Bordell, Chuck **27**
Bradbury, Ray 141
Braun, Mark **28-29**
Brave and the Bold, The 32, 111
Brenda Starr 71
Bridwell, E. Nelson 32
Brigman, George 131
Brown, Chester 99, 167
Brown, Roger **30**
Buckler, Rich 108, 156
Bugs Bunny 91
Burgos, Carl 73
Buscema, John 75, 160
Buscema, Sal 138
Bush, George 27-28
Busino, Orlando 30
Busiek, Kurt 13, **31-33**, 169
But I Digress 53
Butcher, The 111
Byers, Reggie **34-35**
Byrne, John 23, **36**, 95, 138, 160, 167

Caliber Press 19, 24, 27, 38, 62, 76,
    78, 91-92, 102, **166**
Campiti, Dave 96
Caniff, Milt 16
CAPA-Alpha 153, **175**

Capp, Al 98
Captain America 27
Captain America 16, 33, 73, 95, 137, 168
Captain Marvel <u>109-110</u>, 117, 129, 146
Carlin, Mike 115, 162
Cartoonists across America 141, 143, **170**
Cartoonists and Illustrators School [see School of Visual Arts]
Casper 81
Cerebus 18, 105, 169
Cerebus Bi-Weekly 37
Chaos! Comics **166**
Charlton Bullseye, The 117
Charlton Comics 36, 79, 117
Checkmate! 58, 60
Chiodo, Joe 118
Chiron, Sorceress of Loutrell <u>16</u>
Chrislip, Bruce **37**, 170
City of Glass 101
Classics Desecrated 24, 38
Classics Illustrated 68
Claypool Comics 42, 119, 135, **166**
CLG Comics 37, 170
Clopper, Brian **38-<u>40</u>**, 171
Cochran, John **41**
Cohn, Scott **42-<u>43</u>**
Colan, Gene 75-76, 91
Cole, Jack 141
Collins, Terry **44-46**, 170
Colón, Ernie 32
Comic-Book Heroes, The 84
Comic Shopping <u>76-77</u>
Comico the Comic Company 34-35, 45, 91, 105, 129, 135-136
Comics and Sequential Art 130, **173**
Comics and Stories, Walt Disney's 28, 119
Comics Buyer's Guide 3, 18, 24-25, 53, 63, 69, 76, 79, 81, 137, 146-147, **173**

Comics Journal, The 41, 99, 119, 122, 167
Comics Pro Magazine 81, 146, **173**
Comics' Greatest World 88
Complete Crumb Comics, The [see *Crumb*]
Complete Guide to Drawing from Life, The 131
CompuServe **173**
Conan 104
Congorilla 135
Cottonwood Publishing 98, **170**
Couch Potato Newsletter, The 65
Cracked 24, 30
Crane, Roy 16, 100
Crawford, Randy H. **47-<u>48</u>**, 171
Crawford-Chadwick, Meloney 128
Create Your Own Comic Book 172
Creatures of the Id 91
Crumb, R. 122, 168
Crumb Comics, The Complete 167
Crump, Rusty **153-155**
Crusaders, The Mighty 16
Cruse, Howard **49-<u>52</u>**, 167
Crystal Comics 35
Cult Press 91
Cuti, Nick 36
CyberForce 168
Cyclone Comics 111
Cynicalman, The Amazing <u>62</u>-64

Danger Unlimited 36
Daredevil 58, 76, 91, 95, 124
Daredevil: Born Again 101
Dark Horse Comics 31, 36, 54, 56, 61, 68, 78, 88, 112, 114-115, 134-135, 140, **167**
Dark Horse Presents 91, 167
Darkwing Duck <u>104</u>
David, Peter **53**, 167, 173
Davis, Dan **54**
Davis, Rob 174

Days of Wrath 134
DC Comics 13-14, 16, 30-32, 36, 42, 44, 46, 53-54, 58-62, 66, 73-74, 77-79, 81, 83-85, 88-89, 91, 96, 99, 101-102, 104-105, 108-109, 111, 113, 115, 122, 127, 129, 135, 137-138, 142, 145-147, 156-157, 161, 163-164, **167**, 172 [see also Paradox Press, Vertigo]
Deadpool 137
Deathstroke 58
Debbie's Dates 74
DeCarlo, Dan 166
Dechnik, Suzanne **55**
Dell Comics 71
Dennis the Menace 44, 99, 141
Desert Peach, The <u>19-20</u>, 166
Destroy!! 13
Detective Comics 83, 93, 98
Devil Dinosaur 78
Dick Tracy 28, 41
Dinosaurs for Hire 27
Dishman, The Mundane Adventures of 99-100
Disney (general) 28, 61-62, 79, 99, 115, 118-119, 134, 167
Disney Adventures 56
Disney Afternoon, The 119
Disney Comics 31, 66, 104, 121
Ditko, Steve 23, <u>41</u>, 95-96, 111, 135
Dixon, Chuck 96
Doc Savage 44
Dr. Doom 55
Dr. Radium, Man of Science 118
Dr. Seuss 146
Dr. Strange 56, 124, 146
Dr. Who 59
Donald Duck 79, 91
Donald Duck 167
Dooley, Kevin 92
Doom Patrol, The 137
Dorkin, Evan 56, 168
Dragonring 22

Drawing Dynamic Hands 174
Drawing the Human Head 174
Drawn and Quarterly Publications 65, 101, **167**
Dream Corridor, Harlan Ellison's 114
Dreamery, The 19-20
Duckman 169
Dunn, Ben 166
Durante, Jimmy 16-17
Dyer, Sarah **56-<u>57</u>**, 169-170
Dynamic Anatomy 174
Dynamic Figure Drawing 174
Dynamic Light and Shade 174
Dynamic Wrinkles and Drapery 174

E-Man 27, 36
Eagle 35
Eclipse Comics 13, 19, 20, 31, 37, 59, 62, 64, 96, 99, 100, 118, 134, 145
Eclipso 162
Eclipso: The Darkness Within 61
Edlund, Ben <u>44</u>
Eerie <u>41</u>
Egor's Hobby Hints <u>48</u>
Eighth Man 34
Eisner, Will 112-113, 122, 130, 168, 173
El Diablo 83-84
Elflord 22
Elfquest 44, <u>69</u>, 169
Elfquest: Bedtime Stories 86, <u>87</u>
Elfquest: Blood of Ten Chiefs 55, 86
Elfquest: Hidden Years 55
Elfquest: New Blood, 22, 69
Elfquest: Shards 55, 86
Ellison, Harlan 114
Elvira, Mistress of the Dark 135, 167
Endless Gallery, The 102
Enemy Ace 19, 62
Engel, Jim <u>145</u>
Englehart, Steve 81
Entertainment Weekly 65

Entity Comics 69
Epic Comics 112, 114, 118
Erotic Worlds of Frank Thorne, The
129
Ert! 62, 166
Erwin, Steve **58-60**
Eternity Comics 34-35
Eury, Michael **61**
Evangeline 96
Evanier, Mark 154
Everett, Bill 73
Evil Ernie 166
Exhibit 'A' Press 93, **170**
Explorer Press 44, 170
Explorers 44, <u>46</u>, 169
Extreme Studios 168

Fabulous Furry Freak Brothers, The
143
Factsheet Five **174**
Falling <u>147</u>, 170
Fanboy 28
Fantagraphics Books 19, 50, 84, 102,
118, 129, 137, 140, **167**
Fantastic Four, The 52
Fantastic Four, The 16, 19, 30, 36, 47,
55, 58, 62, 76, 83, 95, 108, 114, 127
Father and Son 105, 168
Faucher, Wayne <u>137</u>
Fear and Laughter 68
Feazell, Matt **62-64**, **150-<u>152</u>**, 166,
171, 175
Fever Pitch 38-39, 171
Fiasco Comics 122-123, **171**
Fields, Gary 30
Fighting American 81
Figment Press 27
First Comics 58-60, 62, 78
Fish Police 76
Flaming Carrot [see *Teenage Mutant
Ninja Turtles*]
Flash, The 47, 58, 66

Flash, The 32, 83, 115, 137, 141, 167
Flash Gordon 134
Fleener, Mary **65**, 167
Fleischer, Max 62
Flenniken, Shary 68
Flintstones, The 166
Foglio, Phil 48
Fortier, Ron 86
Foster, Hal 98
Frank <u>140</u>
Frank the Unicorn 141, <u>144</u>
Frazetta, Frank 22, 113
Freedom Fighters, The 16
Friedrich, Mike 86
Funnyman 16
Furrlough 66

Gafford, Carl **66**
Gallacci, Steve 20
Gasoline Alley 28, 141
Geary, Rick **68**
Gen 13 103
Gerber, Steve 154
Gertler, Nat **69-70**
Getting into the Business of Comics
6, 82, **174**
Ghost 61
Ghost Rider 17
Ghost Rider 114, 124
Ghost Rider 2099 124
Giant-Man 16
Giant-Size Dracula 36
Giant-Size Mini-Comics 37, 64
Gibbons, Dave 167
Gill, Tom <u>71-72</u>
Giordano, Dick 32, 89, 163
Gladstone Comics 121, 167
Gold Key Comics 61, 115, 129
Goldberg, Stan **73-75**, 166
Golden, Michael 38
Good Housekeeping 30
Goodies 47

Gorelick, Victor 75
Grahame, Neil 29
Great Expectations 68
Green Arrow 111 [see also Green
    Lantern]
Green Hornet, The 55
Green Hornet, Tales of The 79
Green Lantern 32
Green Lantern 18, 83
Green Lantern/Green Arrow 141
Green Lantern Corps, The 32
Grell, Mike 59, 113
Griffin, Rick 142
Grimjack 58, 60
Groening, Matt 65, 166
Gruenwald, Mark 33
Guardians of the Galaxy, The 131
Guler, Greg 115
Gunfire 58-59
Guy Gardner: Warrior 54
Gwen 56

Haines, Lurene 6, 82, 174
Hama, Larry 104, 134
Hamilton, Tim 84
Hamlin, VT 54
Hanna-Barbera 52, 58, 166
Harlan Ellison's Dream Corridor
    [see Dream Corridor]
Harris Comics 127-128, 167
Harrison, Sol 66
Harvey Comics 61, 71, 99,
Hauk, Steve 76-77
Hawk and Dove 88
Heavy Metal 49, 62-63, 68, 112, 122
Heckle and Jeckle 41
Hectic Planet 169
Helfer, Andy 42
Hellblazer 167
Hellboy 88-89
Hellraiser 114
Hembeck, Fred 154

Henry 101
Hernandez, Jaime and Gilbert 167
Hero Alliance 79
Hero Zero 61
Hester, Phillip 78
Hi-Yo, Silver 71
Highbrow Entertainment 168
Hoest, Bill 30
Hoffman, Mike 127
Hogarth, Burne 174
Hopalong Cassidy 86
Houghton, Jim 84
How to Draw and Sell Comic Strips for
    Newspapers and Comic Books 174
Howard, Robert E. 129
Hughes, Steven 166
Hulk, The 27, 53
Hulk, The Incredible 16, 27, 95, 117,
    123, 168
Hulk 2099 83
Human Torch, The 31, 76
Human Torch, The 16, 73, 107
Hyde-25 167

Icon 168
Images of Omaha [see Omaha]
Imago 27
Impulse 137
Incredible Hulk, The [see Hulk]
indy 146
Infantino, Carmine 83, 109
Infinity Inc. 108
Ingersoll, Bob 79-80, 173
Innovation Comics 44-45, 79, 114
Instant Piano 56, 88
Interview with the Vampire 114
Invisible Man, The 68
Iron Man 27
Iron Man 95
Isabella, Tony 36, 66, 79-81, 173

Jabberwocky Graphix 47
Jacobs, Will 83-84
Jam, The 91, 166
Java Town 118, 168
Jeres, Patricia 92
Jetsons, The 166
Jim 140
Joe Kubert School of Cartoon and
  Graphic Art **175**
John Byrne's Next Men [see *Next
  Men*]
Jonah Hex 16, 113
Jones, Bruce 118
Jones, Gerard **83-85**
Jonny Demon 31, 135
Jonny Quest 58
Journey into Mystery 95
Jughead 77
Jughead 44, 166
Jungle Moon Man 18
Jurgens, Dan 115
Justice League, The 66
Justice League International 83
Justice League of America, The 66

Kabuki 166
Kamandi 16
Kane, Gil 27, 83, 159-160
Kato, Gary **86-87**, 169
Kennedy, Jay 63
Kesel, Barbara Randall **88-90**, 115
Kid Blastoff 56
Kidz of the King 34
Kimba the White Lion 34
King Hell Press **171**
Kingdom Come 137
Kirby, Jack 16-17, 23, 58, 76, 95, 107,
  111, 113, 127, 135, 145
Kitchen, Denis 50
Kitchen Sink Press 37, 50, 105, 122-
  123, **168**, 176
Korak, Son of Tarzan 129

Krusty the Clown 166
Kupperberg, Paul 79
Kurt Busiek's Astro City [see *Astro
  City*]

Lady Death 166
Lang, Jeffrey **91-92**
Lash, Batton **93-94** 170
Last Gasp Publications 143
Latigo 98
Law Is a Ass, The 79-80
Lee, Jim 168
Lee, Stan 83, **95**, 127, 168
Lee, Wendi 87
Legend 36, 167
Legend of Wonder Woman, The [see
  Wonder Woman]
Legion of Super-Heroes, The 153
Legion of Super-Heroes, The 61, 66,
  137, 141
Legionnaires 137
Levitz, Paul 67, 109
Lewis, Richmond 171
Liberty Project, The 31
Li'l Abner 98
Lieber, Steve 92
Liefeld, Rob 108, 168
Life, the Universe, and Everything 135
Lincoln, Abraham 13
Little Archie [see *Archie*]
Little Lulu 49, 99
Lobito, Tony 103
Lone Ranger, The 71
Looney Tunes 30, 91
Lost in Space 44-45, 79
Lost Laughter 105
Loubert, Deni 18, 130
Love and Rockets 56, 132, 167
Lovecraft, HP 45
Lum: Urusei Yatsura 83
Lyle, Tom **96-97**
Lynde, Stan **98**, 141, 170

MacLeod, John **99-100**
Machlan, Mike 108
Mack, David 166
Mad 44, 47, 49, 62, 65, 68, 105, 118, 132, 167
Mad Dog 115
Mad Dog Comics 118
Magazine Enterprises 16
Magic: The Gathering 166
Magnus: Robot Fighter 114, 165
Mahnke, Doug <u>61</u>
Maison Ikkoku 83
Malibu Comics 27-28, 83-84, 115, 135, **168**
Man of Steel, The 36
Manara, Milo 122
Manic Panic <u>132-133</u>
Mantra 168
Marauder 27
Married with Children 28
Marrinan, Chris <u>125</u>
Martin, Don 24-25, 30
Marvel Age 59, 61
Marvel Comics 16, 28, 30-32, 36, 41-42, 44, 46, 50, 53-54, 58-59, 62, 69, 73-74, 76, 79, 81-83, 85, 91, 93, 95-96, 99, 101, 104, 108, 111-112, 114-114, 117-119, 122, 124-125, 127, 129-130, 134, 137, 146, 157, **168**
Marvel Comics Presents 33
Marvel Superheroes 58, 101, 108
Marvel Tales 73
Marvel Try-Out Book 59, 115
Marvel Two-in-One 69
Marvels 28, <u>31</u>
Mask, The <u>61,</u>
Mask, The Adventures of the 61
Mask's Summer Vacation, The 68
Mason, Tom 84
Matt, Joe 167
Mayer, Sheldon 141
'*Mazing Man* 88

Mazzucchelli, David **101**, 171
McCaffrey, Ann 153
McCloud, Scott 4, 7, 8, *13-15*, 31, 64, 100, 130, 160, 175
McFarlane, Todd 168
McKenzie, Alan 174
Medal of Honor 134
Megaton Man 122-<u>123</u> [see also *Savage Dragon, normalman*]
Messick, Dale 71
Mickey Mouse <u>79</u>
Mickey Mouse 31
Mickey Mouse Adventures 119
Micronauts, The 78
Mighty Crusaders, The [see *Crusaders*]
Mighty Mouse 99, 145
Mighty Samson, The 129
Mignola, Mike <u>89</u>, 167
Milestone Media 69, **168**
Milk and Cheese 168
Milke, Joe 131
Millenium Publishing 44-45, 114
Miller, Frank 27, 101, 113
Millie the Model 74
Mireault, Bernie 92, 166
Mr. Jigsaw 86
Mr. Monster 3D 145
Ms. Tree 86
Moebius 122, 144
Moncuse, Steve 76
Moon Knight 79
Moonshine McJuggs 129
Moore, Alan 46
Moore, Dick 141
Moore, Terry **102-103**, 166
Mundane Adventures of Dishman, The [see *Dishman*]
Munden's Bar 60, 62
Murray, Doug **104**
My Girl Pearl 74
Mystery in Space 104, 109, 156

Nakashima, Ken 20
'Nam, The 104, 134
Nancy 101, 140
Nanny Katie 91-92
National Cartoonists Society 68, 72
National Lampoon 68
Naughty Bits 19
NBM Publishing 68
Negative Burn 19, 24, 38, 78, 91, 102, 166
Neville, Bill 44, 46, 170
New Adventures of Abraham Lincoln, The [see Abraham Lincoln]
New Moon Directory, The 155, **175**
New Teen Titans, The [see Teen Titans]
New Warriors, The 124, 126
New World Order 117, 170
Newell, Eddy 81
Next Men, John Byrne's 36
Nexus 78, 112-113
Nice Day Comix 47, **171**
Nice Day Mini-Comix 47
Nicholson, Jeff **105-106**, 168
Night Thrasher 32
Night Wynd Publishing 22
1963 122
Ninja High School 166
Nordling, Lee 121
normalman 130
normalman/Megaton Man Special, The 122
normalman 3D Annual 145
Not Available Comics 62, 150, **171**
Not Brand Ecch 101
Nova 124-125
Now Comics 28, 55, 69, 79, 91
'Nuff Said **175**

O'Neil, Denny 32, 141
Obadiah, Rick 59
Ocean Comics 86

Olbrich, Dave 84
Old Paper 18
Omaha, Images of 37
Ominous Press 112
Onli, Turtel 107
Onli Studios 107
Original Street Fighter, The [see Street Fighter]
Ordway, Jerry **108-110**, **156-164**, 167, 172
Orlando, Joe 42, 109

Pacific Comics 118
Palliard Press 19, 47
Paper Tales 37, 170
Paradox Press 42, **167**
Parody Press 30
Partners in PanDEMONium 38-40, 171
Patrick Rabbit 170
Patsy Walker 74
Peanuts 18, 62, 99, 101
Peepshow 167
Pen and Ink Comics **171**
Penguin and Pencilguin 142
Pensa, Shea Anton **111-113**
Perozich, Faye **114**
Phantom of Fear City 42
Pini, Richard 169
Pini, Wendy 69, 154, 169
Plastic Man 41, 141
Playboy 32, 129
Plump Not Pregnant Comix 132
Pollard, Keith 122
Poorhouse Press 173
Popeye 62
Potts, Carl 84
Power Factor 96
Power of Shazam, The [see Shazam]
Power Man/Iron Fist 32
Pozner, Neal 54, 147, 154
Pratt, Doug 174

Prime 168
Primitives 171
Prince Valiant 28, 98
Protectors, The 27
Pulido, Brian 166
Punisher, The 96, 111 [see also
  Archie, Spider-Man]

Quantum Leap 79
Quasar 42

Radio Ray 16
Radioactive Man 166
Ramos, Humberto <u>137</u>
Rankin, Rich 35, 136
Ranma 1/2 83
Rare Bit Fiends 171
Rawhide Kid, The 16
Read My Lips 28-<u>29</u>
Real Stuff 19, 102
Real War Stories 134
Red Sonja 129
Reed, Daniel **117**, 170
Reeves, George 122
Regulators, The 54
Ren and Stimpy Show, The 44
Renegade Press 130, 145
Retro-Dead 117, 170
Revolutionary Comics 132
Ribit <u>129</u>
Rice, Anne 114
Richie Rich 69
Rick O'Shay 98, 141
Rick O'Shay, Hipshot, and Me 98, 170
Rico, Don 144
Rip-Off Magazine 18
Rip-Off Press 18, 24
Riverdale High 137
Roadways 91
Robin, <u>43</u>
Robin 96
Robinson, Jerry 73, 98

RoboCop 124
Robotech 34, 135-136
Rocky and Bullwinkle 62
Rog-2000 36
Roger Rabbit 104
Roger Rabbit's Toontown 119
Rolling Stone 44
Rom: Spaceknight 78
Romita, John Jr. 138
Romita, John Sr. 75, 101
Rook 127, 167
Ross, Alex 28, <u>31</u>, 137
Rozakis, Bob 13
Rubber Blanket 101, 171
Rubber Blanket Press **171**
Rubin, Leigh <u>144</u>

Salicrup, Jim 61
Samurai 22
Sandman, The 167
Sandman: World's End, The 111
Savage Dragon, The 168
*Savage Dragon vs. the Savage Megaton
  Man, The* 122
Savage Tales 104, 134
Savannah College of Art and
  Design, The **175**
Scalphunter 16
School of Visual Arts, The 42, 71, 73,
  98. 174-**175**
Schreck, Bob 91
Schutz, Diana 45, 91
Schwartz, Julie 32, 138
Scooter 74
Screaming Dodo Studios **171**
Scroggy, David 68
Secret Origins 137
Seidman, David L. **119-121**
Seinfeld, Jerry 7
Self-Publisher **175**
Semper Fi, 134
Sentry 79

Sgt. Fury 16, 54, 95
Sgt. Rock 62
Severin, John 30
Shaboogie 148
Shadow, The 167
Shadow Strikes!, The 83
ShadowHawk 130, 168
Shadowman 114
Shanda the Panda 66
Shatner, William 58, 114
Shatter 60
Shaw, Scott 68
Shazam 146
Shazam, The Power of 108, 109-110, 162, 164
Sheena, Queen of the Jungle 129
Shelton, Gilbert 143
Shetterly, Will 45
Shield, The 16
Shires, Ian 174
Shooter, Jim 108, 146
Shoptalk 175
Showcase 33, 54, 66, 162
Shuriken 34-35
Shuster, Joe 16-17
Silver Star 31
Silver Surfer, The 83
Silvestri, Marc 113, 168
Sim, Dave 18, 105, 130, 169
Sim, Deni [see Loubert, Deni]
Simpson, Don 122-123, 171
Simpsons, The 166
Sin City 103
Sirens 27
Skolnick, Evan 124-126
Sky Wolf 96
Slave Labor Graphics 56, 118, 130, 168
Slaton, Joyce 132-133
Slimer and the Real Ghostbusters 28
Slutburger 65, 167
Small Press Network, The 175

Smith, Jeff 40, 168
Sniegoski, Tom 127-128, 167
Solar: Man of the Atom 165
Sonic the Hedgehog 166
Sorenson, Jennifer 56
Soulsearchers and Company 135, 166
Space Ghost 58
Space Ghost: Coast to Coast 56
SpareTime Studios 171
Spawn 103, 168
Speed Racer (comic book) 55, 70; (TV series) 69
Speedball 126
Spider-Man 23, 58, 66, 95, 97, 101-102, 124
Spider-Man 46, 53-54, 58, 95-96, 109, 124
Spider-Man, The Amazing 81, 168
Spider-Man, Untold Tales of 31
Spider-Man/Punisher 96-97
Spiderbaby Grafix 78
Spirit, The 122
Spoof Comics 30
Sprang, Dick 23
Standard Comics 129
Star Blazers 34
Star Trek (comic book) 79, 115, 123; (novels) 53, 58; (TV series) 124, 172
Star Wars (comic book) 38, 167; (films) 38, 172
Star Wars: Dark Empire 88
Starlog 49
Starman 96
Static 168
Staton, Joe 59
SteelDragon Press 45
Steranko, Jim 76
Steve Canyon 16
Stinz 19, 21
StormWatch 168
Strange Tales 31, 95
Strawberry Jam Comics 18

Street Fighter, The Original 86
Strike 96
Stuck Rubber Baby 49-50, 52, 167
Sugar and Spike 141
Superboy 32
Supergirl 32
Superman 1, 16, 36, 58, 66, 83, 93, 98, 102, 105, 108, 138, 157
Superman 36, 46, 58, 142, 163, 167
Superman, The Adventures of (comic book) 108, 156; (TV series) 122
Superman: The In-Between Years 32
Swamp Thing 46, 78, 127, 167
Swan, Curt 135

Taboo 78, 127
Takahashi, Rumiko 83
Tales of the Green Hornet [see *Green Hornet*]
Tales to Astonish 73, 95
Tantalizing Stories 140
Tarzan the Warrior 135
Technoboy 23, 148
Technoboy Returns 23
Teen Titans, The 109, 153
Teen Titans, The New 88
Teenage Mutant Ninja Turtles 143, 166, 135
Teenagents 31
TekWorld, William Shatner's 124
Terry and the Pirates 16
Third Dimension Comics 145
Thomas, Roy 81-82, 154, 160
Thomas-Fleming, Ronald 175
Thompson, Don and Maggie 79-80, 154
Thompson, Hunter S. 68
Thorne, Dave 144
Thorne, Frank **129**
3D Zone, The 145, **172**
Through the Habitrails 105

Tick, The 44
Tick: Karma Tornado, The 44
Timely Comics 71, 73, 95 [see also Marvel Comics]
Tintin 141
Tiny Toon Adventures 44, 91
To Be Announced 18
Todd, Kathe 24
Tolbert, Matt 29
Tom and Jerry 86
Tomahawk 129
Tonto 71
Tony's Tips 81
Too Much Coffee Man 139, 170
Topps Comics 31, 66, 135, **169**
Torch of Liberty, The 36
Totem 27
Toth, Alex 100, 159, 168
Traffic, Max 175
Treasury of Victorian Murder, A 68
Trimpe, Herb 76
Trouble with Girls, The 83-84
Truman, Tim 96
Tundra Publishing 140
Turner, Ron 143
Twilight Zone, The 55, 91
Ty Phoon 98
Tyler, Rurik 30

Ultra Klutz 105-106
UltraForce 83, 168
Uncanny X-Men, The [see *X-Men*]
Uncle Jam 143
Uncle Scrooge 68, 121
Uncle Scrooge Adventures 167
Underground 78
Understanding Comics 7, 8, 13, 15, 100, 130, 160, 172, **175**
Understanding Minicomics 62-63
Underwater 167
Unknown Soldier, The 16

Vado, Dan 118, 162
Valentino, Jim **130-_131_**, 168
Valerio, Mike 84
Valiant Comics 114, **165**
Valor 137
Vampire Lestat, The 114
Vampirella 167
Vampirella, Vengeance of 127
Van Zyl, Kate **_132-133_**
Vansant, Wayne **134**
Veitch, Rick 171
Veronica 137 [see also *Betty*]
Vertigo 102-103, 111, **167**
Vick, Edd 20-21
Victory Comics 34-35
Vigilante 58, 60, 79
Village Voice, The 49, 65
Viz Communications 83
Vokes, Neil **135-136**, 167
Voyage to Veggie Isle 170

Waid, Mark **1**, 33, 61, 84, **137-138**,
  163, 167
Walt Disney's Comics and Stories
  [see *Comics and Stories*]
Wandering Star 171
Ward, Jay 62
Warp Graphics 22, 44, 55, 69, 86,
  169
Warren, Jim 41
Warren Publishing 41, 167
Wash Tubbs 16
Watchmen 88, 114
Watts, Eric 155, 175
Wein, Len 67
Weirdo 65
Wells, HG 141
Wendel _49_
Wendy Whitebread 122
West, Adam 61, 122
West Wind Publishing 173
What If? 33

What The-?! 30
Wheeler, Doug 24
Wheeler, Shannon **139**, 170
WildCATs 168
Wildlife _66_
WildStar 108
WildStorm Productions 168
William Shatner's TekWorld
  [see *TekWorld*]
Williams, Keith _61_
Wilson, Ron
Wimmins Comix 65
Winged Tiger, The 141, 170
Wizard: The Guide to Comics 69, 172,
  176
Wolff and Byrd, Counselors of the
  Macabre 93-_94_, 170
Wolverine _77_
Wolverine 53
Wonder Color Comics 96
Wonder Man 83, 115
Wonder Woman 109
Wonder Woman 36, 167
Wonder Woman, The Legend of 31
Wood, Teri S. 171
Wood, Wally 113, 122
Woodring, Jim **140**
World's Finest Comics 28
Wright, Gregory 124-125
Wrightson, Berni 22
Wuthering Heights 68

X-Factor 53
X-Files, The 169
X-Men 1, 34, 66, 112
X-Men 36, 46, 95, 124, 137
X-Men, The Uncanny 168
Xxxenophile 19, 47-48

Yeh, Phil **141-_144_**, 170
Young Indiana Jones Chronicles, The
  115

Young Love 81
Youngblood 138, 168
Yronwode, Cat 96

Zap Comix 65, 142
Zeck, Mike 117

Zen: Intergalactic Ninja 69
Zero Zero 101
Zone, Ray **145**, 172
Zorro 169
Zot! 13, 14, 62, 64
Zot in Dimension 10-1/2 62, 64

PRO MOTION

HOW TODAY'S CREATORS BROKE INTO COMICS.... AND THEIR ADVICE TO YOU!

...Makes an excellent gift for the aspiring comics professional or *any* fan of the comics world! To order additional copies from the publisher, postpaid, just send a check or money order in US funds for $17.95 per book [$19.00 in Pennsylvania, including sales tax] from anywhere in the US or Canada to:

BOARDWALK PRESS
PO BOX 362
WYNNEWOOD, PA 19096-0362

CREATORS!

If you'd like to share your anecdotes and advice in a future edition of *ProMotion*, please contact the author at Boardwalk Press, PO Box 362, Wynnewood, Penna. 19096

About the Author

Brian Saner-Lamken, a graduate of Oberlin College who has
cartooned for more than a decade under the pen name "Blamken", is
a lifelong student and scholar of the comics medium. He has written
extensively on comics for a variety of publications, including *Comics
Buyer's Guide*, and authored the introductions to the *X-Men* and *Spider-Man*
volumes in the Marvel Comics Postcard Book series from Running Press.
He currently serves as an editorial cartoonist for *Comics Pro Magazine*
and produces *comicScrypt*, the weekly newsletter of Fat Jack's Comicrypt,
through his own Sweet Potato Studios. Brian's self-published comics
work includes *Falling: A 24-Hour Comic* and the graphic novel *Reunion*.
He was last spotted in the suburbs of Philadelphia talking to his cat.